ANSWERS TO THE MOMMY TRACK

ANSWERS TO THE MOMMY TRACK

How Wives and Mothers in Business Reach the Top and Balance Their Lives

Trudi Ferguson
and
Joan S. Dunphy

NEW HORIZON PRESS
Far Hills, New Jersey

Library of Congress Catalog Card Number: 90-62417

Trudi Ferguson and Joan S. Dunphy
    Answers To The Mommy Track

ISBN: 0-88282-062-1
New Horizon Press

CONTENTS

INTRODUCTION

This is a book about women who have reached the top of their professions but who still describe themselves as mothers first. One woman with whom we talked symbolizes the attitude of the others by saying that if it was a question of her children's welfare it would be no question; she would give up her business (a most successful medical practice) and move to the desert on a moment's notice if that was what was needed.

The notion that women have to make a choice between work and family, or that institutions are not responsible for redefining success to include women who decide to have children, or that there is something immutable about organizational life which requires women to choose between work and family, is insidious and distressing.

The debate which has erupted over the article entitled *Management Women and The New Facts Of Life* by Felice Schwartz, president of Catalyst, in the January/February 1989 *Harvard Business Review*—interpreted as suggesting that women who want to be mothers should be placed on a "Mommy Track" and choose whether their careers or families come first—brings up serious issues for women of the 1990s.

The respondents in this study are women who are fully capable of making significant contributions at the very top of any hierarchy and in any arena. It has not been demonstrated that one has to work at 120 percent continuously during a lifelong career to arrive at adequate positions of comprehension or achieve power. Women who are both career oriented and mothers can choose to attend to their families, to meet organizational demands and to conduct business if they have to—sometimes with children crawling on the floor—and still be key players in the important decisions of institutional and business life. Most of the women in this study defy the inference that mommies are second class professionals and they *decry* and are maddened at the notion of the "Mommy Track."

Schwartz discusses two tracks as "career-primary" and "career-and-family" women. According to the article, "career primary women then are required to remain single or at least childless or, if they do have children, to be satisfied to have others raise them." The career-primary women have made a choice early on that career is most important to them "that they put career first" and "they are ready to make the same trade-offs traditionally made by men who seek leaderships positions, to make sacrifices in their personal lives to make the most of every opportunity for professional development." Schwartz outlines strategies for corporations to deal with women who are "among the best managerial talent you will ever see." The strategies call for clearing a path to the top for them with early identification, equal opportunity and equal expectation for travel and relocations and (the one accommodation) recognizing that the business environment is more difficult and stressful for these women than for their male peers.

However, Schwartz sees the majority of women falling into the other category of career-and-family women, "women who want to pursue serious careers while participating actively in the rearing of children." Most of them, she feels, "are willing to trade some career growth and compensation for freedom from the constant pressure to work long hours and weekends." For these women, Schwartz outlines policies and practices institutions can provide, such as: flexibility, freedom to take time off, part time employment, and job sharing.

The recognition for which Schwartz calls, about the differing roles and needs of women, is crucial and the elevation of the discussion of conflicting demands on women is a significant contribution. But, many contemporary women have demonstrated that they are "career-primary" and are still excellent mommies.

It is for those women that this book was written; those who are unwilling to accept the terrible dilemma of an either/or decision in which they either forsake seeking the top of their professional field or the significant rearing of their children, and those who will, in the future, choose both business and family life.

For such women even the term "career-primary" causes difficulty. If, as some of us believe, life is a totality, then we are intellectual, sexual human beings, and our minds and hearts cannot be separated or doled out, but must work together. It is the essential job of the healthy human being to find and maintain a balance of these functions in life. When we are hungry, we eat. When we are tired, we rest. When we are dulled, we stimulate ourselves. We adjust and readjust to minute and to grandiose changes in an attempt to keep our human equilibrium. In professional careers there may be extraordinary demands that make us "career-primary" for a limited period of time, or family-oriented for others.

In the pages which follow, you will meet women who are extremely dedicated to career goals but simultaneously demonstrate the great lengths to which they will go to be responsible to family commitments. For instance, Carol Dinkins was a woman who was offered what she viewed as a once-in-a-lifetime opportunity to serve as Deputy Attorney General. She agreed to leave her husband and young children for four years in Texas to assume this position. Perhaps this was a career-primary moment. It certainly was a tough choice. But during this period she boarded an airplane every weekend just to be with her family and to maintain her own commitment to them. It is true that she was able to do a difficult job because she had the financial wherewithal and support to arrange for the proper care of her family, but increasingly we find the "red eye special" full of career-primary women racing home to their children.

Today there are hard choices that both women and institutions make in balancing their competing demands. But the successful women interviewed for this book, plus more and more successful mommies/businesswomen, make these choices and accept their consequences daily.

An unfortunate implication of the "Mommy Track" argument is the notion that institutions should be accommodating to women's issues. But the realities of childbirth and childrearing warrant more than token accommodations granted by the "ruling class." It would be preferable to refocus future discussions on granting women real power to define their lives, their institutions, their psyches and their ambitions.

There are women who are committed to both work and family roles. There are women who have raised, or who are raising, decent children and who have also achieved great professional success. How have they managed? Who are these women and how did they arrive in their positions of power? Who raised their children? Are they different from older successful women? What are their backgrounds, personalities, supports, models, strategies, obstacles, tips, problems at home and at work? What are their prescriptions for success? Where have they found entry and respect in organizational life? These are the real questions which women of the 1990s need to focus upon and answer as they make their own lifestyle choices.

There is a mega-message in the "Mommy Track" theory that follows a dysfunctional, but often typical, female pattern that internalizes guilt and blame. It is that somehow the innate condition of woman makes her responsible for these distinctions and problems. But gender is not the fault of women; it is a given, not a choice, and women do not have to assume the responsibility for compensation. Instead they have to learn more about the way the world is and the way their psychology works, and create new scripts for themselves (about what is appropriate) and for institutions (about what success and hard work is like). Control of their powers, competence in their distinct styles, and confidence in the legitimacy and health of fulfilling their needs will serve to promote better internal and organizational balance than new forms of segregation.

CHAPTER ONE

THEN
AND NOW

"We are here to stay."

Dianne Arnold
—Executive Vice President
First Bank National Association

We can look first to social and historical factors that have contributed to women's acceptance in the marketplace, particularly to a new set of female behavior and skills.

Domestic life in this country has changed, and work is no longer done primarily at home. We have moved away from agricultural societies in which women made a significant contribution at home. During the transition, women's social influence was reduced, or at least rechanneled, almost exclusively into child rearing. At the same time, families were having fewer children. This factor, coupled with technology, resulted in new family dynamics. As time went on, more single and divorced women were supporting children and the economy often necessitated two incomes. Therefore, many bright women felt, if they had to work, they might as well make it interesting and worthwhile.

At the same time, women were becoming increasingly well-educated, which is both a symptom and a cause of change. Roles and social dictates are constantly reinterpreted, depending on need. (For example, women serve in the Israeli army because they are needed.) World War II created a need for women in the workplace. Married or single, women went to work because men were fighting a war. As a result, social norms changed.

More changes were to come. The civil rights movement reinforced the focus of feminists on disparate treatment and raised new options about the roles and competency of women. The women's movement provided a forum for public discussion of very personal roles and raised the consciousness of both men and women, as well as organizations. Public policy statements have also become supportive of women, and such statements are now continually reinterpreted to coincide with change.

The legal system has mandated some changes through affirmative action and equal opportunity. The requirements of those programs, coupled with improved census and data-gathering techniques, provide continuing impetus for change. Statistics are now available on the number of working women, their positions, comparative salaries, and discrepancies in promotions and raises.

Our social philosophy and governmental system also have begun to support meritocracy and fairness, lending further credence to the women's movement and creating opportunities for women to progress on the basis of performance rather than gender. Several women in an accounting firm specifically cited their work environment as particularly receptive, one which rewarded women on the basis of performance. They felt there was ample opportunity for women to work to their potentials and plenty of room at the top.

Along with equal opportunity programs, other government systems, such as the courts, have helped reformulate our collective conscience regarding women and minorities. In enforcing the programs and laws that mandate equal opportunity, the government further endorses a public policy of intended support. A recent court decision involving an Atlanta law firm, King & Spalding, upheld a ruling that federal antidiscrimination laws are applicable to partnerships even in the selection of new members of the firm. Although it was applied to law firms, the principle sends warnings to accounting, architectural and other large firms as well.

In many instances, the government has stipulated the hiring and promotion of women as a requirement for engaging in business. These governmental standards mandate a change in the way companies have formerly done business. Increased receptivity is fostered through controlled loans, aid, task force studies, and such organizations as the Small Business Administration.

All this has resulted in changes in the available work force and changing expectations. A new pool of workers introduces new values. If institutions are to survive, they must accommodate the reality of these changes.

Many of the women in this study, who have created and seized these new opportunities, have demonstrated they are competent in previously untested areas.

Any attempt to understand the relationship between femininity and success in today's work environment must account for the experience of the previous generation of women who entered professions before there ever was a Women's Movement. They were the true pioneers who made changes for the next generations of women possible. They broke barriers. Then the Women's Movement provided stimulus for a more concerted effort by a younger generation. Both of these forces have opened new doors and served as models for work styles to follow. The contrast between older successful women and contemporary successful women is, if analyzed, instructive.

Much of our knowledge about women who realized their success before the '60s is derived from the seminal work done by Margaret Hennig and Anne Jardim, two former Harvard Business School professors who published their academic research in a popular book, *The Managerial Woman.*

This book, published in 1976, is still widely read and is generally considered a key source of information for women intent on becoming successful in business today.

Based on their research, Hennig and Jardim included in *The Managerial Woman* suggestions about appropriate behavior for aspiring female managers. First of all, they said, a woman should plan her career with long range goals in mind rather than simply taking jobs as they come. They recommended she adopt a masculine style of dress and behavior and be more restrained emotionally in the working environment.

The results of the Hennig-Jardim research was later amplified by two recent surveys of successful women in business. One conducted by Korn-Ferry International, in conjunction with the UCLA Graduate School of Management, compared executive females with their male counterparts. A majority of the women ascribed their success to producing results, assuming responsibility, and demonstrating a positive attitude. But, like the Hennig-Jardim group, these female managers said that the greatest obstacle in their progress was simply being a woman.

The other survey, done by the *Wall Street Journal* and the Gallup Organization, said essentially the same thing. Female corporate executives employed by companies with more than $100 million in sales confessed to the problem of balancing home life and work life, and two-thirds said they had made significant personal and family sacrifices for the sake of their careers. Eighty percent said there were disadvantages to being a women in the professional world. (Interestingly, only twenty-five percent said they, themselves, had been stymied on the way up the corporate ladder because of being a woman.) More than half said they had consciously changed their personalities by becoming less emotional and more businesslike in order to succeed at work. The statistics indicated that the majority of the women were unmarried and without children.

On the basis of the Hennig-Jardim research, a profile emerged of the prototypical successful woman of this era. She was from a stable home environment and had a close relationship with a father who served as a role model. She went to college, but not to graduate school, took her first job as a secretary and enjoyed the close sponsorship of a male boss. She either never married or married late in life, had no children and worked at the same company all her life. On the job she suppressed her femininity and relied on her technical skill for advancement.

In contrast to the Hennig-Jardim study of older successful women, our research, which has had a different emphasis, yielded very different results.

During the last decade, one of our authors, Trudi Ferguson, surveyed women from a younger generation, educated in a more encouraging environment with more personal supports, and demonstrating the acceptability of combining work and family life. In contrast to Hennig-Jardim, Korn-Ferry and WSJ/Gallup, the successful women interviewed were, on an average, forty years old or younger, married and with at least one child. They were also chosen from a wider spectrum of professional life so that the experience of non-managerial women could be compared to that of successful business executives who worked in a presumably more male-dominated culture. They were exceptional women who demonstrated that there were other ways of being successful than acting like outsiders, emulating men, and denying themselves the pleasures of family life. They forged a new path that would point the way for others.

The profiles presented in these pages draw on three different studies. Their results build upon one another. The first was an examination of highly successful women born around 1950. This generation had felt the pulls of career and family and the conflict about what were deemed appropriate roles as they entered the work force as young women.

Contemporary young women of this generation certainly shared different historical circumstances than the older pioneering generation. They grew up with the Women's Movement and Betty Friedan's *The Feminine Mystique*. Their fathers were confronted by the opportunities and changes in their own daughters' lives. Many of their mates and brothers were socialized along with them and have had to work with them in redefining these roles. These life differences influenced women who now approach the 35 to 45-year mark. One of them, Trudi Ferguson, wanted to find out how others felt. Her first study was based on in-depth interviews with fifty highly successful women and explored the factors they felt were keys to their success, the obstacles, their backgrounds, role models, supports, reasons for working, definitions of success, and differences from men.

Interviews were followed up by administering an Androgyny Scale and Personality Questionnaire, the details of which will be discussed later.

The women with whom she spoke were drawn from a variety of fields: law, medicine, science, management, entertainment and art. They earned an average of over $100,000 a year. This was an extraordinarily diverse group ranging from the first female captain of a 747 (a thirty-three year old petite and quiet woman), to the tall, energetic founder of a multimillion dollar chocolate chip cookie empire. She met with the director of a successful jazz tap ensemble, the chief executive of a major metropolitan children's hospital, high level corporate managers, reporters, television newscasters, Hollywood producers, surgeons, judges and successful artists.

As a result of this study, she began to do more work as a management consultant, working with women in organizational life. Unfortunately, she found that many of the married women studied were not enjoying complete success, either as women with children or as executives. They complained about the need to hide their true identity. One woman described her work voice and her weekend voice. Many said they didn't talk at the office about children they had or those planned for the future. They felt unappreciated and overlooked. Very often they left their organizations.

Some of these very organizations called her for help. They complained that women were leaving in large numbers. She was asked questions about what to do and why was this happening.

As a result of these inquiries, she began a second study on retention rates of women in organizations and what happens to women who don't enter the upper echelons of the highly successful executive branch of business. She tried to find answers to questions such as what was different about them or their institutions. Mainly, she found that these women were saying that they work differently and the way in which they work is unappreciated— unlike successful male executives. In response to her questions, they asked questions of their own, such as "how could they be themselves and still succeed?" Organizations asked how they could retain these women.

As Trudi describes it, "While I was doing most of this work I was young and single . . . but getting older. At thirty-eight, I married. At thirty-nine, I had one child and, at forty-one, I had a second. My research followed my personal dilemmas as I began to ask questions about how women manage success and children. In the recent past I saw the baby boom generation begin its debate on the 'Mommy Track.'

"The discussion distressed me. I was a mommy, but I didn't want to be on a 'Mommy Track.' At this point, Joan Dunphy, the president and publisher of New Horizon Press, and I got together. She, too, was married, had children, was career-oriented, and offended by the idea that women who married and had children should be sidetracked in their careers. Would I be interested in investigating what was happening to women in top management who had families? I was—and so the concept of this book was born.

"We decided to revisit the women in both earlier studies who had become mothers. The main questions we wanted to ask were:

- Had motherhood limited their professional achievement?

- How had they overcome 'Mommy Track' dilemmas?

- Did they have emotionally healthy children?

- Did they forsake their own families?

- Did they self limit due to family constraints or the constraints of their own psyches?

- What were the lessons to be learned from mommies who had made it?

- What could they teach individuals and institutions about women's own skills and opportunities?"

In addition to revisiting Ms. Ferguson's original respondents, we decided to include additional women who were both mothers and top professionals. We were also anxious to talk with some women from earlier generations to see how their life experiences differed from present generations'.

Thus, the women represented in this book combine re-interviews from Ms. Ferguson's original study of highly successful women (eliminating those who were not mothers), additional contemporary working women (successful and mothers) and a few women from earlier generations who might add further insights to our present and future search for family and work success.

Finally, we chose to avoid the pitfalls of poll-taking and question-and-answer surveys. Pen and paper tests offer a different level of disclosure than in-depth probing. Like Margaret Hennig, we wanted to conduct extensive interviews to get a sense of the traits that characterized each individual and to see how much they differed from previous generations and from the images in our popular culture. Each of the women interviewed was unique and fascinating in her own way.

However, a small number of women were surveyed in-depth due to the representative qualities they conveyed. These women include:

*Doreen Braverman—Head Lawyer for Writer's Guild, married with one child.

*Lita Albuquerque—Los Angeles artist and gallery owner, married twice and currently married with two children and pregnant (at 44) with her third.

*Dianne Arnold—Executive Vice President, First Bank National Association, married with two children.

*Cathleen Black—Publisher *USA Today*, married with one child.

*Helen Blumin—Internist in private practice in Santa Monica, married with two children.

*Barbara Boxer—Congresswoman, married with two children.

*Elizabeth Blalock—Neurologist at Kaiser Permanente, two children.

*Yvonne Burke—Former Congresswoman, attorney, married with one daughter.

*Marcy Carsey—Co-owner Carsey-Werner Productions, married with two children.

*Barbara Corday—Former President of Columbia Pictures TV, one daughter and two stepdaughters.

*Sandra Day O'Connor—Supreme Court Justice, married with three sons.

*Carol Dinkins—Partner in a Texas law firm; former Deputy Attorney General of the United States, married with two children.

*Susan Estrich—Law Professor at the University of Southern California; campaign manager for Dukakis For President, married with one child.

*Debbie Fields—President and CEO of Mrs. Fields Cookies, married with four children.

*Marjorie Fine—Surgeon in private practice, married with two children.

*Nancy Evans—Former Publisher of Doubleday, married with one child.

*Dr. Anna Fisher—Astronaut and doctor, married with two daughters.

*Pam Flaherty—Vice President of Marketing and Development at Citicorp, New York, married with two children.

*Rebecca Sinkler—Editor-in-Chief of *The New York Times Book Review*, married with three children.

*Sharon Flaherty—Senior Vice President at Kaiser Permanente, married with two children.

*Ellen Gordon—President of Tootsie Roll, Inc., married with four children.

*Gail Koff—Founding partner of Jacoby & Meyers, married with three children.

*Madeleine Kunin—Governor of Vermont, married with four children.

*Jennifer Lawson—Executive Vice President, PBS, one child, one step-child.

*Nancy Schort—Dentist in private practice, married with two children.

*Amy Roseman—Gynecological surgeon in private practice, married with two children.

*Geraldine Ferraro—Lawyer, former candidate for Vice President of the United States, married with three children.

*Cherilyn Sheets—Dentist in private practice, married with one child.

*Merrie Spaeth—President of Spaeth Communications, married with one child.

*Debbie Smith—Vice President for Xerox, married with two children.

*Marcy Tiffany—Regional Director Federal Trade Commission, married with three children.

*Julia Thomas—Chairman of the Board of Bobrow/Thomas and Associates, an architecture, planning and consulting firm and past President of the Committee of 200, remarried with one daughter by a previous marriage.

*Karen Warren—Chief Operating Officer of the City of Hope, three children.

*Martina Whitman—Vice President of General Motors; formerly on President's Council on Economic Advisors, married with four children.

*Peggy Noonan—Author and former presidential speechwriter, one child.

These women, and the others represented, wear coats of power in many and differing ways. Through their efforts, doors that once were described as hopelessly locked have opened, and many other women have gone through them to take newly opened positions at top salaries. They are creatively forging new identities for married working women with children.

In this book they share their experiences of how they avoided the "Mommy Track" and stayed on the main line to success without forsaking healthy family lives.

CHAPTER TWO

BACKGROUNDS FOR SUCCESS

"Growing up on a ranch, I learned about independence and taking care of my own needs."
Sandra Day O'Connor
—Supreme Court Justice

Diversity is the main theme in the backgrounds of the women interviewed. Some of them began life in poverty and deprivation; others grew up with every luxury. Some started with all the obvious societal advantages; others had nothing to guide them except their own imaginations. This wide diversity of backgrounds was instructive, because it reinforced our theory that there is no single pedigree necessary for those destined for success. The range of these backgrounds confirms broad access to achievement.

There are no strict generalizations one can make about what constitutes the "typical" curriculum vitae of the successful professional woman. Nevertheless, there are several common threads that recurred among the women in this study such as great vicissitudes, opportunities, love and the development of autonomy.

First, many of them confronted early hardships such as a family divorce, the death of a parent, or an emotional trauma that had a lasting effect on them, providing the impetus to launch a successful career.

One who faced this kind of challenge is Jennifer

Lawson, Executive Vice President of Public Broadcasting Corporation. Her mother died when she was thirteen years old and she had to learn and plan for herself. She has done much traveling alone working with a variety of people and the resulting positive experiences "gave me something else to build on . . . so when I felt failure, it wasn't so devastating. It was just for the moment." Lawson's mother was a professional school teacher who married late and had her first child at thirty-eight. She was miserable after she married, since she could only substitute teach and, therefore, felt wasted as an intelligent person. The home did not offer enough of a challenge for her. Jennifer's father was an unconventional auto mechanic/inventor, who encouraged her in things which were not typical girls' roles. "I learned welding and minor auto repair. I had an older and younger brother and two older stepsisters, and everybody learned the same things."

These early survival skills contributed greatly to her later success.

"I see my close women friends who are so destroyed by one failure."

Jennifer lives with her second husband, her stepson, and their six-year-old son. Her child was born when she was thirty-seven years old. She has always wanted children, but felt her personal circumstances were precarious and, as she says, "I wasn't going to have any by myself." She had been with PBS for a number of years and in her present job for three years when her son was born. "The workplace is important, and I worked up until the day of delivery . . . I went home and my son was born later that night. I took six weeks maternity leave, but we were in the funding cycle, and I did go into work one or two weeks after he was born. I brought him with me and nursed him even though there was heavy traffic. I amused friends with my *Do Not Disturb* sign on my office door.

"Of course, I have moments of stress and difficulty. The greatest anxiety is finding good quality day care. The day care I wanted had a waiting list of over two hundred fifty children. I made the decision I wanted day care rather than in-home care as I thought my child would get more attention. I remember the horror of having to take a three week old baby out to be "reviewed" because I had to go back to work and needed a responsible facility in which to leave my child. At six weeks, he entered day care 7:30 a.m. to 6:00 p.m. I had no guilt because the center was very good, and I was coming home to a healthy, happy baby. There was comfort in that I was well informed of what was going on. For example, they kept a log of what the baby had eaten!"

Asked if she felt conflicted by the urgent work demands and any residual impact on her softer side, she said, "I don't feel violated by my profession. I play many roles with friends, husband and children and am comfortable moving in and out of them."

Interestingly, the biggest difficulty for her was adjusting to the complexities of corporate life. Her corporation comes under siege every three years as it is financed by Congressional funding and that opens the opportunity for critics to make known their problems. It is stressful for the people within the organization. There is a struggle between independent producers and the station, each claiming discrimination.

But, significantly, Jennifer said she didn't feel any current problems as a woman or Afro-American or as a mother. "Maybe it is part of my own constitution. Certainly there have been past circumstances when people were trying to take advantage of me. In 1975, I found that my rate of pay was lower than that of a man doing comparable work. I immediately raised that issue with my employers, saying if they didn't raise me I would have to quit." They increased her salary.

In her first job with a church, Jennifer was warned by several friends and the secretary that she would be working for an extremely sexist and racist man who would constantly refer to her as his "gal." Jennifer told him if he used "gal," then she expected she could use "boy." She made it crystal clear exactly how she expected to be treated.

She feels the 1990s workplace is shifting to the role of the neighborhood with longer hours. Close friends and social and professional life have to shift to be more flexible. "If you have terrific people, you make allowances. Both PBC and CPB have been very supportive about child care with tax credit, and it is a supportive place for families. If, on a snowy day, I bring in my six year old, he is treated with fun and charm, and others have brought in their children.

Jennifer's husband respects her independence and is very supportive. "He has an interest in being non sexist. He is excellent in management of the household and care of the child. He is an excellent parent."

But the difficulty is that they *both* have extremely demanding schedules which continue to extend longer than each anticipated. "Each month I try to plan the calendar, but sometimes there are pangs such as a meeting that caused me to miss the school play. Even though my husband went, it was painful. Though I don't even think my son missed me. Still, I missed being there, but I don't feel guilt, just regret."

Her new job involves a lot of travel. "But once this smooths out, things will be different." Her tips to aspiring women, "I have a computer terminal with a modum to the office. That way I can be the Mom at home and cook dinner, and when I need to work overtime I can do it at home, so I can be a physical presence. She believes in rituals like "vacations and special holidays and special weekends and dinner together and reading to my son before he goes to bed. I'm clear about my goals and creating a *future.*"

Her determination is amazing. Despite multiple pulls on her energy and time, every other year, she said, "I take a short vacation alone to look at who I am and where I want to go." Last year, she took a beach house by herself for a week. "I think about the cities I would like to live in, and jobs I'd seek, and what is important to me. It's a coming to grips with how I am and what I really want. Now I am focused on creating harmony in life: a mixture of work, family and friends. I care about public television and think I would like to spend the next three to five years making a contribution, but then I would like to take a sabbatical to do some writing, and then maybe enter teaching. I want to focus on history and life."

According to Lawson, "Combining roles is a matter of individual choice. You decide what is most important. You don't have to halt your career. It is certainly possible to do both."

Jennifer had a wonderful comparison. "Sometimes I think to myself, 'How much time does Queen Elizabeth spend raising her children?' Nobody asks what is she doing. I simply focus on harmony and balance."

Twenty-five percent of the women in this study had difficult childhoods. Two had mothers who were institutionalized for mental illness and died when their daughters were still young. Geraldine Ferraro's father died when she was eight. "One day he was perfectly healthy and the next day he was dead and my world fell apart."

One movie executive's father died when she was nine, and she witnessed her mother's ordeal of suffering and her subsequent release—through a new-found commitment to work. Lita Albuquerque was an illegitimate child, who never even knew her father. Raised in a convent with her brother, she knew her mother only as the woman she could visit during summer vacations.

Aside from death, abandonment and divorce, many of the women documented strained relationships with their parents. Astronaut Anna Fisher's mother immigrated from Europe. Her father joined the army before he graduated from high school and later worked in a warehouse. Anna was the first member of her family to graduate from college.

Some of the other women had family hardships

that, depending on the individual, could have served as a source of either inspiration or despair.

Clearly, poverty or family turmoil could have crippled any number of these women for life. Yet they responded to adversity in classic Horatio Alger style by channeling their energies in a positive way. However, beginning in their formative years, some developed the feeling that somehow they were outsiders. Because of their looks, their family circumstances, or their imagined inadequacies, quite a few considered themselves exceptions to the rules that supposedly governed little girls growing up in their generation.

Poor Self-Image

A number of the women described their physical attributes in a way that set them apart from their more bountifully endowed peers. They commented on their self-images as motivating forces in their successes. Dr. Amy Roseman had a vivid memory of her "bigness" through adolescence. One executive used two words to describe herself as a young girl: big and fat. Another woman who exuded glamour and sex appeal found it hard to forget that she was skinny and awkward as a child. In her view, she was not cute when it counted, and the impression stuck, long after her looks changed.

A producer remembers being a social outcast as a youth, who retreated into her own special world. She had no social life and spent her time taking dance, skating and music lessons. "It didn't seem like a big denial," she says, "since I was scared to death of being social. I wasn't popular. You have to have something if you aren't having a good time." One of her biggest satisfactions in life came when she returned to her high school for her twenty-year reunion, right after winning an Academy Award. She had never been one of the "stars" in her class, but, that night, her classmates greeted her, this one-time "nobody," with a reception line. For her, it was definitely sweet revenge.

Many women did not feel part of the mainstream,

so they turned to other venues in an effort to build confidence and credibility.

Positive Themes

By no means did all the women in this study have childhoods that were uniformly dreary and unhappy. In fact, a common theme, even among those who suffered early traumas, was the fact that someone, usually, but not always, a parent, was there when they were needed. No matter how severe these young girls' troubles, they felt there had been someone to love them and offer support. Almost all the women described being raised in an environment where they had a feeling of being valued by an adult. Especially for those who felt deprived in other ways, the influence of this supportive figure was crucial and lasting. They were the ones who clarified the confusion the women felt as girls, and who helped by pointing them in the right direction.

There were, of course, women fortunate enough to have been born with certain advantages and opportunities, including two loving and supportive parents. One lawyer felt free to go to law school because she had parents who believed in her and were happily willing to financially support her education. Business executive Ellen Gordon was given not only support, but also major opportunity when her father gave her the top job at his company, Tootsie Roll.

Debbie Fields, of Mrs. Fields' cookie fame, was able to borrow money, as well as get good business advice, from her husband to launch her first business. He also had exceptional business expertise as a financial manager. He was a Stanford graduate who had already established a reputation as a financial expert. So, she had an intimate accomplice who had the education and seasoning to augment her naive enthusiasm.

Other successful women did not have these fortunate types of opportunities, but they made their own opportunities and succeeded.

A Parent's Positive Guidance

Elizabeth Blalock, an attractive blonde who could easily be a fashion model, is a practicing neurologist, well respected in her field, who half-jokingly, half-candidly states that her career development was the result of good genes and good programming. "I never was encouraged to be first in an athletic event. I was pushed into academic excellence instead. From a very early age I was programed, and this is the result."

Her father was a successful urologist, who, during Elizabeth's childhood, returned to night school and received an additional law degree. He was the dominant figure in the family—the leader. He loved his children, but also made it clear he didn't like it when they performed less than perfectly. Among other things, he made sure that Elizabeth and her siblings lived up to his expectations and achieved their potential. His children were rewarded for progress in school and punished if they got less than good grades. Elizabeth respected her father, but, at the same time, feared him. She felt his approval was the most important thing in the world. She was strongly encouraged to assume responsibility for fulfilling her potential.

When Elizabeth reached the age of thirteen, her father began introducing her around as "his daughter, the future urologist." By the time she reached her late teens, it was obvious that her only brother did not want to be a physician, so Elizabeth's father redoubled his efforts at encouraging her. He got involved in all the details of her life, including advising her on what classes she should take in high school.

Elizabeth's mother worked intermittently as an actress, but her husband was critical of her career, because the theater was non-academic. For her part, her mother disparaged housework and encouraged Elizabeth to make sure she kept her options open. The message Elizabeth got was this: "You are your own person. Don't be dependent on a man."

Part of her mother's concern grew out of a sense of frustration. Her marriage was unhappy and her choices seemed circumscribed. Elizabeth's home life was stormy, until her parents finally divorced when she was fifteen. During high school, she lived in New York City with her mother, but she moved in with her father during her first year in CCNY. He subsequently moved to Georgia, and Elizabeth followed him. Georgia turned out to be more fun than New York, and provided her with more of a social life. Then, with one year remaining in college, she married a successful businessman who was six years older, as a way of "creating my own family."

Her brief respite affected her grades and, as a result, Elizabeth failed to be accepted into medical school. Instead, she enrolled in graduate school, studying biochemistry, and started medical school in another community. She lived in a dormitory from Monday to Friday, working diligently so that she could transfer to a university closer to home. Initially, her husband was supportive of her studies, since it was "a feather in his cap" to have a future doctor for a wife. She felt being married during medical school was comforting, especially since she was one of the few women students. The fact that she was "attached" was a convenient protection when male classmates teased her or engaged in some harmless sexual advances.

However, her circumstances changed dramatically with the arrival of her first baby. Suddenly, her husband wanted her at home. He didn't even want Elizabeth to finish her residency, and it was over his objections that she continued her schooling. After a second child, a daughter, was conceived, their relations grew more tense. Apart from everything else, he resented the power that went with her status as a doctor, and they finally divorced in her seventh month of pregnancy after eight years of marriage.

Following her divorce, Elizabeth moved with her children to California and accepted a position with Kaiser Permanente's health plan organization. "I assumed I would behave in the same way I had during my training, but, when I did, problems developed." The other doctors told her she was too aggressive and shot from the hip, which made her angry. "I felt I was just being honest. I am not afraid of anything or anybody, and I express it. If something moves me, I have a strong reaction; I have firm ideas on what is right." Apparently her strong opinions were not that objectionable since she eventually received a promotion to Chief Endocrinologist.

Dr. Blalock feels that being a female doctor keeps her on her toes. She has to keep her antennae tuned, especially to incipient power plays. "I never considered myself someone who strives for power, but I learned there is power in being a woman. Because early on I looked up to men and wanted to lean on them, this has been a great disappointment. But, then, I have learned to use my power and femininity to soften things when I have to be aggressive or critical. I've also learned how to use my gender to my advantage to smooth situations. However, I am afraid that in dealing with more unpleasant aspects of wielding power, I have developed a cool, aloof manner. When men get to know me, they are often surprised to find me sweet."

Elizabeth, for all her success, would like to be married again. She says she enjoys the feeling of family even though she likes the option of making all her own decisions and not having to answer to anyone.

At this point, she primarily works, she says, "to support my family." On the other hand, she feels a little like an explorer who has conquered a mountain and wants to go on and find new terrain. She insists, "I love my work, but it is sometimes a little too hectic. Some of the challenge is gone. I've done it so long and I want to try something new."

Still, she finds it hard to break the pattern of obsessive work that was established for her as a child. A classic example occurred on a two-week European trip. She had rented a car and looked forward to a glorious drive through the south of France. The only problem was she simply couldn't relax. She actually felt relief on the day she lost her wallet, since the task of reporting her loss provided her with a challenge.

During the trip, however, Elizabeth made a change that gave her a different challenge. She relinquished the post of Chief Neurologist. When she moved to a new office with different work perimeters, she took action that would ensure her a better life.

Development of Autonomy

A distinguishing characteristic of the majority of these women was the capacity for exercising independent judgment. According to some researchers on female development, a trait that distinguishes many successful women is a sense of autonomy. This quality has been defined in three ways. A woman with a sense of autonomy has the capacity to cope with being perceived as unconventional, is not dependent on others for what she thinks and feels, and is capable of reinforcing her actions with positive feedback of her own.

Successful women develop a sense of autonomy. They have already adjusted to being different in their younger years. So it is not a "new experience" when they move toward a high level of success, because they are already used to being in a so-called "man's world." All during their lives, these women develop internal standards of validation. Many of them discovered their own uniqueness early on, and found sources of support for their atypical patterns.

The women who felt as though they were outsiders, due to disadvantages or opportunities, were already prepared to exercise the emotional self-reliance required for their steep climb up to the highest reaches of the professional ladder. Many of those women who grew up feeling a part of the mainstream had seen themselves as leaders. Either way, these women needed a strong sense of themselves to exercise the resilience needed, not only to survive, but to flourish.

Background Information

In the Hennig-Jardim study of successful women, it was found that every single one of the female executives profiled was an eldest child. Indeed, it is a popular belief that the first child in a family is more likely to be the most successful adult. However, in our study, only a slim majority were the first born in their families, and there was nothing to suggest that second or even third-born children were less likely to succeed. They didn't offer confirmation of the stereotypical view, that, for example, oldest children were necessarily more responsible and controlling or that middle children were usually compromisers and peace makers.

Interestingly, among the most successful women we studied, only a few had been only children. It is fair to speculate that growing up with brothers and sisters prepared many of these women for the give-and-take required in the real world.

Marriage and Mates

Only half of the executives interviewed married in the Hennig-Jardim study, and most of those did so late in their careers. By contrast, the vast majority of the women in our new study were married by the time they reached twenty-five. Half were married at the time Trudi first met them; the rest married in the time between her first and second studies. Thirty-five percent had been divorced, but many of these had already remarried when we reinterviewed them.

AGE OF FIRST MARRIAGE

(First set of Interviews)

Age	% of Women
Before 25	77
26–34	13
35 or older	10

DIVORCE AND REMARRIAGE

Divorced	35%
Single Now	15%
Second Marriage after 35	20%

Education

Although the majority of women had devoted a large percentage of their lives to attending college and professional schools, almost a quarter had never graduated from college. Generally, these were women in business who didn't need any credentials. Debbie Fields and Barbara Corday, two of the most successful respondents, did not have college degrees.

By limiting the population of our follow-up study, we chose to reinterview only women with children in order to find out how they succeeded in business.

Reasons for Working

What motivated these women to enter the work force? In order to understand successful women, it is important to understand the basic reasons that drove these successful women to work. This specific question was asked of each participant in our survey.

The vast majority said they work neither for money nor prestige, but for stimulation. Their language offers clues about the intensity of their drive. "I work because it gives me the most pleasure in life." "My husband and child are very important and they are what makes it all worthwhile, but without my work, I disappear." These are two common responses. The women we studied enjoy dealing with people, making decisions, and feeling they are at the center of things. An accountant, stinging from her firm's perception that she might leave to devote all her time to her second child, said her superiors had it wrong: "I came to work when my baby was one-and-a-half. I know what it's like to work and care for a child and to stay home."

Those women who did cite financial reasons for

working expressed a need to contribute to family requirements, a desire for independence and to prove they could
take care of themselves. Some said they took a job to support their families but, as long as they were working, they
wanted to make the most of career opportunities.

Nevertheless, whether the motivation was necessity
or accomplishment, the significant financial contributions
made by these women in particular, and working women
in general, fundamentally and profoundly affects the well-
being of the family unit and it affects their self images both
in terms of independence and control.

Ultimately, *strategy* is something you improvise. An
example is Merrie Spaeth, former vice president of Republic Bank, who, in a period of ten years, went from obscu-
rity to being a national figure. At age thirty, she decided to
return to school. Her story gives us faith that it is never too
late.

Selected by *Glamour* magazine in 1985 as one of the
ten outstanding women in the country, it would not be
stretching a point to say that, in the case of Merrie—an
expert in the emerging field of communication—real life
has imitated art.

In 1964, Merrie Spaeth played "Marian Gilbert," one
of the two schoolgirls whose unbridled imaginations had a
great effect on other people in the popular Peter Sellers'
film *The World of Henry Orient.* Twenty-six years later, she
is still impacting people with the fruits of her imagination.
For instance, according to *The Washington Times* (Decem-
ber 25, 1984), while she was a Special assistant to President
Reagan, "Ms. Spaeth took the White House Office of Media
Relations into the computer age . . . with an electronic information system to . . . transmit all White House news
material . . . directly into subscribers' computers or word
processors." Additionally, the newspaper reported, "She
initiated the office's use of space satellites, making direct
access to President Reagan or other senior administrative

officials available to local television stations around the country."

A few years before, she had been Special Assistant to the Director of the Federal Bureau of Investigation.

Merrie resigned her Washington position at the close of 1984 to become a vice president at the Republic Bank in Texas, one of the largest bank holding companies in the United States.

What is interesting and ironic about this remarkable (and striking) energetic woman is that in her teens all she aspired to was a schedule so busy that she wouldn't be bored. With the good luck of being in a successful motion picture at age fourteen, she continued acting in television and films until, as she told a Washington, D.C. reporter, "in a wonderful moment of sanity, I decided to go to college." She graduated Smith College in 1970 with a B.A. cum laude, made the Dean's list and won a prestigious poetry prize, after which she got married, "because that's what you were supposed to do."

During the three years of her first marriage, she worked as a reporter for *The Philadelphia Inquirer,* edited a neighborhood newspaper in the same city, wrote regularly for *The New York Daily News,* the *Family Weekly* and *Today* magazine and, for a year, wrote speeches for William Paley, the founder and chairman of CBS, in addition to running for state representative in Philadelphia (she lost) and accepting writing assignments from Gold Key publications.

"In my early twenties, I wasn't *committed* to working the rest of my life. I didn't want to end up like my mother. In fact, when I took a psychological test for my reporting job at *The Philadelphia Inquirer* and the tester told me I was full of drive and aggressiveness, my predominant emotion was embarrassment. It wasn't until after the marriage ended and I was in my late twenties that I began to realize I would work for the rest of my life. By the time I was thirty, I was ready to *commit* to work, which meant to me developing a strategy about what I would work at the rest of my life."

Merrie went back to school—the Columbia University Graduate School of Business—and earned a Master's Degree in 1980, made the Dean's list again and received the Achievement Award.

"It was all that steady working which had given me the self-confidence. You're a different person when you have to get up every day even if you're not happy. If you're unhappy with your work, you either have to restructure your job or get a new one.

"There are a lot of pluses for women in the very areas which are considered negative—like the fact that so many men in hitherto exclusively male domains don't take females seriously. Women can sneak up on men, so to speak, or sidle around them without arousing the wariness or irritation that would be another man's lot if he tried it. That worked for me when I conceived of up-dating media communication at the White House with electronic equipment and space satellites to service small city newspapers and local television stations. When I tried a hard sell in the White House establishment, I met with a myriad of negative reactions, so I sort of sidled around the power bases, tiptoed past the red tape and sneaked the project into existence before anyone realized what was happening."

Initiating space satellite communication between smaller stations and the White House "because local television news has expanded so dramatically," was what the press reported Merrie was most proud of during her stint there.

"Of course, even if I had started ten years earlier," Merrie consoles herself, "I mightn't have proceeded any faster. In those days, the top brass wasn't ready for women in their ranks. Now, they think it's neat being a woman. It's easier to get on someone's appointment schedule and easier to get them excited if an attractive young woman comes in. If she has a concept she's excited about; they get excited."

Merrie thinks her job pattern, with many career changes, is typical of the changing times. The highly paid job at Republic Bank in Texas happened just as the bank was going belly up. She left because "the guy who recruited me was passed over for an important job, and that meant curtains for me. The person promoted was a guy who liked numbers, and we were not going to be a good match. That scared the willies out of me. It was so depressing—the thought of going back to work for a big bureaucracy."

She went into business with a married couple; it didn't work out. She left—or was asked to leave—and had to go out on her own. At the time, she was pregnant with her first child.

How did she feel children fit into the picture: "I always saw myself having children, but the time never seemed right. When I came back to Texas, I thought that was the time, but it was not that easy to become pregnant. It was not just another project to knock out."

She is now forty-one, with a two-and-one-half-year old son and a live-in American Nanny. "You have to have excellent child care when, like me, you have no family in the area."

When Trudi first talked with her, she felt especially stressed between running her company and her husband's campaign for Attorney General of Texas. "I feel physically sick and just exhausted and a little scared as the campaign is sopping up so many resources." Tex, her husband, left his law practice at that point. Merrie's business, a communications consulting firm which provides communication courses all over the country, was the sole support for the family.

Her biggest problem was the unexpected crisis—the dishwasher breaking down, the baby's need for a doctor on the Nanny's day off—but the rewards are wonderful. Of her marriage, she says, "We have a real partnership."

Her tips for other women include "try to plan; you have to keep going. Maybe you should get your education first and not feel pressured into having kids. Getting old in your thirties is nonsense.

"In marriage, you have to look at yourself as a full partner. I would like to spend more time with my child and more time volunteering, but I am the financial support now. Still, I am planning a well balanced future. I am realistic enough to know when you want everything, one thing you don't have is time.

"Women have to demand the opportunity to be business women, to have families and to have a husband's support. I have high expectations and so should other women."

Data Summarized

The background data presents a picture of great diversity and there is a difference between the older and younger women in our study. Older women had children earlier and took off more time—years instead of months. They had more children. They appear less angry and more grateful. We aren't sure if that is the result of their personalities or their age, maturity and experience. They are also farther from the frenzy of raising small children. Younger women have more diversity in patterns of early or later marriage and children. They take much less time off work —averaging 11.6 weeks a year. Twenty-seven percent have children after thirty-five; 15 percent have their husbands as the primary nurturer; 12.5 percent have equal responsibility.

These women moved around a lot and changed careers, with 13.8 years the average length of time in their present career and 5.3 years the average length of time in their present jobs—but many only three months. The statistical data makes important points about their histories.

Background Information

(Final set of Interviews)

10%	Currently single
35%	Divorced

10%	Married after 35 for 1st time
30%	Had children before career
27.5%	Had first child after 35
15%	Husband is primary nurturer
73.5%	Mother is primary nurturer
12.5%	Equal responsibility
11.6 weeks	Average time off for children
12.5%	Picked career with children in mind
.075%	Didn't finish college
.175%	Didn't go straight on to school
13.8 years	Average length of time in career
5.3 years	Average length of time in present job
40%	Had mothers that worked
25%	Had difficult backgrounds
35%	Mates in the same field
22%	Mates earn more
67%	Significant Job Change
50%	Changes careers
47.5%	Relocated

CHAPTER THREE

PERSONALITY PROFILES OF SUCCESSFUL WOMEN

"I came from a lucky perspective."

Peggy Noonan
—Presidential Speechwriter/Novelist

Although the women surveyed share the common element of success, their personalities are extremely varied: for instance, Sandra Day O'Connor was calm, balanced, contained and formal; Geraldine Ferraro was fast, roaming, revealing and emotional; Cathleen Black was frank, humorous, flexible and outgoing; Peggy Noonan was optimistic, literate, sensitive and compassionate.

Each woman was asked the same set of questions in the same order and style, but each answer and the resulting profile compiled was unique. Yet some common traits, behaviors and attitudes significantly stand out. The most striking commonality in all these women is their energy.

It is this one quality which catalyzes all their lives. Several of the women used metaphors to describe the explosive pace they felt they have maintained in their professional lives and the tremendous stamina it required. One dentist recalled, "the beginning of my career was like holding on to a rocket." And an import-export executive described her frantic pace as "chasing a carrot."

Taken as a group, focus, ambition and achievements are driving forces in their lives. The women have done things like work day and night, cancel planned vacations or camp out in their offices for nights at a time. One executive worked so hard for so long that she once made a New Year's resolution to indulge in at least one fun thing during each week. A television writer and producer moved to a beach front setting an hour away from her office to break the habit of mingling her work and personal life. "I used to just sleep on my couch at the studio." Lately, she has promised herself she will not work weekends. A Wall Street analyst said she worked seven days a week for five years straight.

In the main, these women were matter-of-fact about the amount of effort they had invested in their careers. To them, it was given, in much the same way education, competence and luck were. Basically, they thought their drive was to be expected of anyone with serious career ambitions, and did not particularly make them unique.

After hearing the description by Dianne Arnold of her many activities and commitments—full-time, top-level work, intense community involvement, board of this, and board of that, Trudi asked her, "then who says you have to prioritize and give things up?"

"You have to do that yourself," she answered, smiling.

We are sure she was frank and truthful but, after compiling so many case histories, we are convinced that these women did extraordinary things and expended enormous amounts of effort to reach and sustain their goals.

The most dramatic theme that emerged in almost all our studies of the personalities of these women was their use of feminine behavior as a key to their success. This is an important and startling finding revealed earlier by Ms. Ferguson and differs from the conclusions of prior studies by researchers on successful women which tended to show them imitating men's styles.

On a recent consulting visit to the offices of a major Wall Street firm, author Ferguson noted men and women executives there dressed almost exactly alike. The females were in basic-hued suits, with little silk bows resembling ties. Their only concession to fashion was an occasional pair of high heels, but even those were shed at lunchtime in favor of jogging shoes. The same pattern of unisex dressing for success even prevails at some of the Hollywood studios, although the dress is a little more casual there for both men and women.

In contrast, this study indicates that women who conform so clearly to masculine styles, although success oriented, often confine themselves to certain levels in organizations. Despite this new finding, many women launching their careers today are still convinced that they not only must look like men, but act like men as well. However, the successful women in this study found that not to be true. The successful breakout women established their own styles. In fact, seventy-eight percent of the women felt that women's work behavior is and should be different than that of their male counterparts.

According to them, men often have more aggressive demeanors distinguished by strong voices and a willingness to take risks and confront issues directly. Effective women set a quieter and more conciliatory tone, asking polite questions, working toward compromise, and developing friendships that they use as reinforcements for their actions.

As well as showing feminine sides, many of the women in this study identified feminine traits as keys to their successes. For example, Amy Roseman finds that being a female obstetrician is being an obstetrician in demand. According to her, a number of women prefer to be treated by a female physician, and, since there aren't too many of them, the ones in practice are very popular.

A noted businesswomen originally found women in

her field an "unknown quantity." She felt the novelty value of being female was a great help. She didn't have to fight any stereotypes; as the first women in her company at a high ranking level, she could dictate her own rules. This situation allowed her to be straight forward. She told the management, "You guys don't know what to do with me so let me offer a few suggestions."

A computer program manager says that she doesn't feel inhibited by expectations she will act "just like a woman." Instead she plays off them. "Women are not expected to be rational," she says. "So when I am, it seems even more significant."

Several of the women studied said they were unwitting beneficiaries of the changing attitudes toward women. They were able to capitalize on the sudden attention paid to affirmative action and the women's movement. One who heads her own organization said, "I find being a women gives me an edge. Nobody took me seriously for a while, but by the time they did, I was ready."

Marcy Tiffany, head of the FTC says: "It is an advantage being a woman. It disarms the adversary and charms your friends. Women can take advantage of the fact that there is a bias against women. Many men don't prepare much and it gives a competent woman an edge. They are underestimating an adversary."

Feminine Intuition

An extremely successful advertising executive, whose agency bills in excess of $20 million annually, feels that a vital element in her success is her psychological intuition. "I have a sense of what makes people go; I know people's hot buttons. I know how to pitch business. I never delude myself that we are better or smarter than our competitors. But often we get accounts because I know what clients want and what they will respond to. Some respond to praise, some just want the facts, and other respond to money or power. The fact that I pay attention to that important dynamic has to do with being a woman."

One entrepreneur attributed her success to her intuitive abilities, which throughout her life she had been allowed, even encouraged, to develop. "I trust my intuition and, as a result, there are almost no wrong turns." Being a woman, she says, has been a plus. "It is easier to develop a strong male side than to develop a strong female instinct. The women I really like are closer to being perfectly androgynous than men."

The myth prevails that women should conceal the emotional sides of their natures in the professional world. Many of the women in this study, however, disclosed that being able to tap their emotions was indispensable in their work.

Rating Femininity

In an effort to understand the self concept held by these successful women regarding their own masculinity and femininity, Trudi administered a test, devised by psychologist Sandra Bem, known as the "Bem Androgyny Scale." Most women surveyed took the test immediately following her interview. The test consists of characteristics which have been tested on the general population. In those tests, hundreds of men and women were asked to rate themselves on a scale of one to seven, from "never" to "almost always," if they could envision themselves when they heard phrases such as "loves children" or "makes decisions easily," or "shows compassion." The lists included the general words, "feminine" and "masculine" for self-assessment. The responses from the test provided norms against which anyone can be measured.

Bem numbered one end of the rating scale plus $+1$ for feminine, the other minus -1 for masculine. Women in general seem to scale themselves somewhere around $+.43$ or about midway in the femininity section where we would expect to find them.

Mean Androgyny Rating*

Scale	Group Means
Feminine +1.0	
	Bem's Norm +.43
	Norm of Working Mommies in this book −.40
Androgynous 0	Norms of successful working women with or without children −.717
	"Most" successful women −.960
Masculine −1.0	

*0 is Androgynous. Positive scores are feminine: Negative scores are masculine.

We noted from the results that these women rated themselves higher than the general population of women for masculine traits such as aggressiveness, self-sufficiency, independence and ambition, thus producing a "masculine-rating." But they also rated themselves high on feminine behavior, including femininity, loyalty and understanding.

Our findings after administering this test of personality traits indicated that the successful women interviewed felt certain adjectives were particularly appropriate when describing themselves: active, direct, self-confident, intelligent, pragmatic, realistic, reactive, happy and competitive. To a lesser extent, they considered themselves attractive, reflective, security-minded, sociable, self-starting, risk-minded and satisfied with their careers. Finally, they were relatively unenthusiastic about describing themselves as either likely to fantasize about other jobs, or being sensitive to difficult sexual demands or pressure on the job.

The findings further revealed that many of the subjects considered their mothers to be more ambitious, competitive, expressive and self-confident than their fathers, and less passive. They saw themselves more like their mothers than their fathers.

In general they saw themselves as intelligent, confident, happy and successful; thus confirming those studies that indicate there is a high correlation between high self-esteem and superior performance. On the other hand, they contradicted the conventional wisdom about the difficulty most women have in delegating tasks or using informal channels of communication, not to mention the common assumptions about the widespread existence of sexual harassment on the job. The message from these women was that they feel capable and directed and can handle themselves in difficult situations and, for the most part, feel good about themselves.

The More and Less Financially Successful

One of the purposes of this study was to attempt to identify the specific differences between more and less financially successful women. Obviously all the women were above average in earning power. They were all successful, yet there were interesting differences between the women in the top group and the others. The table which follows shows the differences in background between the most, more and less financially successful women.

Characteristics of Women in Earning Categories As Revealed on Personality Orientation Questionnaire

Characteristics Rated Higher by Women Earning More

- Being direct in expressing ideas and observations

- Concern with ideas rather than socially appropriate behavior

- Time thinking about career

- Delegating

- Having a mentor

- Being adventuresome

- Feeling capable of holding a top job

- Feeling successful

- Risk Taking

- Fantasizing about other jobs

Characteristics rated high by women earning less

- Satisfied with career

- Importance of physical appearance on their career

- Need for security

- Being sociable

- Having colleagues respond personally rather than to ideas without regard to personalities involved

- Giving up more for their career

A few significant trends can be noted here. Only one of the most successful women was from a single-child home. Most benefitted by learning the social interaction that comes from having siblings. They were also less inclined to stress the importance of hero figures or mentors.

Some of the most financially successful women had husbands in the same professional field, and they talked repeatedly about the importance of their husband's professional comradeship and support.

Meanwhile, the most successful women were also less satisfied than those women earning less. This was either because they were congenitally dissatisfied or because dissatisfaction and impatience are qualities that appear to drive the most successful to their goals.

While seeing themselves as primarily feminine, the most successful women also rated high on the majority of the listed characteristics on the Androgyny Scale that were

considered masculine. They view themselves as more active and more versatile than the women earning less. Specifically, they rated higher on qualities like self-reliance,
competitiveness, willingness to take a stand, and willingness to act as a leader. Women earning less rated higher on
being helpful.

The Personality Orientation Questionnaire indicated which characteristics were rated by the members of
the different financial groups as applicable to themselves.
The characteristics they rated differently were noted and
are described in the Table.

Specifically, the Table shows that in comparison to
the less successful group, women in the most successful
group are more apt to describe themselves as being direct
in expressing ideas and observations, of being more interested in ideas heard objectively rather than socially appropriate responses, being adventuresome, feeling capable of
holding a top job, and comfortable with risks and fantasizing about opportunities.

The women in the less successful group, on the
other hand, are more likely to characterize themselves as
being satisfied with career, preoccupied with the effect of
physical appearance on their career, more security conscious, sociable, and having colleagues respond personally
to ideas rather than objectively.

Although the less successful group felt they were
giving up more for their career, on the whole they felt
more satisfied.

There are four important implications of these findings. The first is that successful women may use—or feel
free to use—natural, feminine skills that they have learned
and cultivated. The second is that successful women credit
personal social skills as key factors in their success. Such
findings should encourage the development of those skills
in others aspiring to succeed. The third is that our findings
dispute past notions of success and create a new model
which incorporates a more legitimate sensitivity. Recipro-
cally, since professional success has traditionally been as-

sociated with men, the increase in the number of women achieving success using feminine skills changes the perception that success has to be linked to masculine behavior. Fourth, that feminine women can and do use typically masculine traits and still retain their femininity.

For women, acting feminine on the job relieves the problem of trying to act in an unfamiliar way. Moreover, organizations and institutions may begin to welcome more balance, understanding, sympathy and sensitivity in the work place as they begin to assimilate the knowledge that such traits are linked with success. As these feminine characteristics have a reciprocal impact on the work environment, there could be a reduction of some of the unhealthy competitiveness and single-mindedness that is characteristic of many offices. The office environment will be enriched by the infusing of more warmth, expressiveness, sympathy and openness.

This is an exciting time. Institutions and corporations are opening their doors to more and more females. If success doesn't have to be drawn from one masculine model, future entrepreneurial women may be free to act in manners that naturally suit them. They may spend less energy learning to act tough or aggressive as did most businesswomen in the past. For instance, one woman with whom we talked said she knew as a child that she could not advance herself with the "normal" things like "looks"; so she had to work hard to develop some other characteristic. Her aggressive demeanor serves her well today, but in the new environment such facades may be less successful. In fact, most of the other women with whom we spoke have capitalized on their femininity. A studio executive translates her sexual attractiveness into non-threatening personal charm which works well in the movie industry. One subordinate described how this woman conducts a meeting by making eye contact with every individual and "working the room."

These women have found they can not only be successful, but be themselves. Women's new successes in behaving naturally and the appreciation by employers of those successes permits a potentially wider range of positive feminine behavior patterns in the business world.

Being Different Is Okay

In an era in which most women in business sought to emulate men's styles, how did these women have the courage to express their femininity? Even when they had been able to capitalize upon it, what made them feel free to discuss it so openly?

Our findings suggest two possible contributing factors. First, these women treading new paths could no longer unthinkingly copy the behavior of their fathers and employers. They either had to set up their own unique guidelines, or they had to choose qualities to admire and emulate from many differing sources.

Second, while performing supposedly masculine duties unlike their predecessors, they felt the need of support and intimate personal relationships, and these, according to many, validated their femininity. Unlike the career women of yesteryear who stood alone, without the support of husbands or men friends, our respondents revealed that having supportive men, at least in the background all along their way, made it easier for them to express their real priorities.

Traits

Other traits remain that are shared by many of these women and offer clues about the ingredients promoting their successes.

It was uncanny how many expressions of speech recurred in women so different, women ranging from demure to earthy. The commonalties were startling. Very different women used the same words to describe their philosophies and strategies.

These same thoughts or ways of handling problems were seen in serendipitous duplication in their vocabularies, their words of wisdom, and what they stress as guiding principles. Many women shared a common concept: "there are no wrong roads." This is a liberating notion enabling women to move, decide, act and experiment. It is a forgiving and comforting idea supporting more varied decision making and actions. One statement made by such diverse individuals as an airline pilot and an architect, as well as a CEO of a Wall Street firm, was to "be the best you can possibly be."

Qualities perceived as important by the first group of women author Ferguson interviewed may be seen in the following table.

Factors Women Perceive as Influencing
Their Success

Percentage of all Noted Factors*	Factors Contributing to Success
48%	Personality and Social attributes
10%	Effort and Hard Work
10%	Being Female
8%	Well Suited to Job
6%	Competency/Ability at Task
6%	Support
5%	Role Models
3%	Working Conditions
2%	Luck
2%	Education

*rounded to the nearest percent.

The qualities mentioned by this group of women more often than any other were friendliness, charm and the ability to inspire the efforts of a group. For the purpose of discussion, these traits have been grouped together as "social skills."

SOCIAL SKILLS

Getting Along with Others

"I am successful because I get along with people aside from being accomplished and prepared. I like people to like me. When you're dealing with the government, they have all the cards, but people like me are more willing to listen and hear new perspectives. Being effective depends on sharing information, going to lunch, cooperating, and making people more conversant with my views, so they will integrate those views in laws," said one executive.

Emphasizing the importance of personality in achieving success, other women in different fields expressed similar sentiments. A West Coast artist and owner of several galleries saw this social dimension as equally important to her achievement:

"I tell my students, if there are two artists with equally good work, but one has a major personality problem like being too pushy, a client will choose the work of the other one."

If you are basically easy to get along with, she explained, and clear about what you want, you get more opportunity. What's more, she thinks it is especially important for younger artists to articulate what they want and to project it effectively to their audience. In short, "Others have to have faith in the artist beyond what you can do when you are first starting out. Curators and gallery people have to use intuition in promoting you. You have to seem bright enough to do interesting work. They want the value of your current work to go up and their judgement in you to be confirmed over time."

Friendliness

Friendliness, a quality not often thought of in connection with business, ranked high in our respondents.

One diminutive woman has a spacious office and a job with big responsibilities. In her thirties, she is a senior vice president at a multimillion dollar entertainment industry conglomerate. Currently responsible for programing and production for daytime television, she joined the company as an evaluator of educational programs after teaching school for several years, and rose to her present position after only three years on the job.

She is forthright and direct, but never abrasive. She has a sparkling sense of humor. She gives the impression of being outgoing, and her co-workers consider her a pleasure to be around. Her friendly, open manner belies her position of power and authority. She is accessible; her office door remains open. She also feels her friendliness helped get her where she is.

Next door to her is the office of her superior, a lawyer who runs the important business affairs division of the company. He is a big man with a formidable presence who wields great influence within the organization. His management style is to dispense information very carefully to the individuals he works with, meting it out in a controlled manner.

When she moved into the office next to his, he developed the habit of dropping in at the end of each business day to sit down and chat. Because of her engaging personality and warmth, he started treating her as a friend rather than a business competitor. In the course of their conversations, he revealed a great deal of business information he might otherwise have guarded very carefully. She acted in her instinctively receptive way and gained his confidence. She says candidly, "I made friends with him in spite of himself."

During these informal sessions, she acquired a lot of useful knowledge which she might not have gotten through conventional channels. It became an enormous source of power for her. Unlike others in the organization, she was aware of projects before they were officially announced, and she was able to anticipate, design responses and have much more influence without ever having to betray her colleague. Instead, she behaved in her own way, providing him the satisfaction of having a receptive friend and confidant, while using the valuable information and association she garnered to her advantage.

It was surprising during our interview to hear her give primary credit to her own personal characteristics. We assumed she would enumerate her job skills, her experience, and her years of preparation. Instead, she pointed to her natural friendliness as a key factor in her success with her company.

In contrast to successful women of previous eras who had to abandon their natural feminine personalities in order to win approval, women like her feel they can put their own personality assets, their often unique feminine attributes, to work, without damaging their chances for advancement. In fact, just the opposite occurs.

Likewise, in responding to questions about major influences on their careers, these successful women credited talents traditionally utilized by women to keep marriages and homes running smoothly—talents which have been thought to be less than valuable in the rough-and-tumble corporate world.

Sensitivity

A disproportionately high number of women in this study placed a high premium on sensitivity. Most respondents found it invaluable to be able to use their instincts to detect how the people they worked with reacted to their ideas and methods of operating, so that they could adjust accordingly. They said it helps, in business especially, to be able to "take the temperature of the room" so that you can sense where you stand with an important group.

A successful accountant said that by using a sympathetic ear and heightened sensitivity, she can get more information from a client, and produce an improved work product for the firm. She adds that she can function more effectively if she draws out information beyond mere nuts and bolts explanations. This talent to gather information arises from her ability to pay attention, respond and to act intuitively, and take in subtle non-verbal clues. These help her to establish good rapport and to form more solidly based appraisals.

Sensitivity can also serve to engender good will among clients or customers. The chief executive officer of a large metropolitan hospital described a situation in which an architect came in to make a presentation before the hospital board. In the course of making his proposal, he offered an obviously misguided appraisal of the requirements of the project while at the same time proposing a design that made sense. Most of the people in the room wound up trying to make the visitor feel like a fool. The woman presiding sensed the situation, and interceded. As a result, the architect saved face while she saved his plan. The ensuing compromise worked out to the satisfaction of everyone.

Facility

Another indispensable social skill which has traditionally been viewed as feminine, now, according to these successful women, clearly serves them on their road to success. It is the art of finding consensus where none seems to exist, and inspiring cooperation among colleagues on the job. The head of the real estate division of a large entertainment corporation reported that she encounters many people whom she feels are brighter than she, but her skill at bringing people together is put to good use so that she can make good deals. She has a sense of who will work together, and ways of ensuring that certain combinations of people will create the chemistry needed to close a deal.

A successful lawyer described her involvement in a tense negotiation in which two sides had become polarized

over a small, but significant point. The talks had deterio-
rated, and the other negotiators at the table, all men, were
prepared to give up and leave the room. At the last moment, she saw the threads of a possible compromise. "Just
a minute, gentlemen," she broke in, "I don't think the numbers are that far apart." The comment, delivered in her
calm but quiet female voice, defused the situation. The discussions were reopened and the deal was made.

The women in this study are sensitive to the impact
of their social skills on the job market and spent much time
freely talking about it.

An executive story editor said, "it is more than luck
and hard work. In my case it was a smile, the ability to get
along with people. I have a pleasant personality and have
survived three regimes. I certainly didn't make it on contacts because I didn't have any."

Many of the women also conveyed that they relied
upon other related social qualities to advance their careers.
They mention the use of charm, diplomacy and flattery.

An artist reflects: "It is hard to say what is the quality that makes you better. I am kind of arrogant and try not
to come right out and say it, so I try to be as charming as
possible, I am reasonably good with people."

An eye surgeon describes a key to her success as
being "noncontroversial" and not making waves in general
but performing her specialty her way.

The other things these women said were useful included the art of listening well, of taking an interest in
others, the ability to offer support and feedback to their
peers and a willingness to assume leadership whenever the
situation required.

Openness and Optimism

These women were all bright, alert, responsive and
enthusiastic. They were open and willing to explore patterns in their own and other women's lives. They were articulate and thoughtful. They were unguarded in using

their own personal experiences to explore new ideas and theories.

They were positive in their outlooks on life. They were optimistic and generally described themselves as happy. They did not dwell on difficulties. They saw most problems as equations to be solved and not as barriers to their progress.

There was little concentration on obstacles to their success but rather in overcoming road blocks and moving on. It could be that being successful makes these women more optimistic, but it appears from their past histories they were that way before they achieved their success. Certainly their optimistic views contributed to reducing barriers.

In explaining their reactions, rather than be felled by discrimination, they would say, "what's all the fuss?" or "that will change with time." If the men they encountered felt reservations about women's abilities, that was "their (the men's) problem."

Upbeat Attitudes

In both personal lives and careers, for instance, these women would forge ahead. Wanting families, they did not see this desire as a career impediment. They had their babies, and then dealt with the consequences mostly, but not always, in optimistic and buoyant manners.

It became apparent that if women in this study hadn't had positive outlooks on life, they easily could have been crippled by a variety of formidable circumstances such as difficult upbringings or external obstacles to their careers. Instead, nearly all these women demonstrated strong resilience that prevented them from being thwarted by serious problems.

In discussing their private lives, many of the women interviewed referred to some difficulties in managing dual roles, but said they were not overcome by the conflicts. Rather, they dealt with such problems by using flexibility and imagination. They made the necessary accommodations and moved on. Sometimes temporary solutions were used, but these women were willing to continue to investigate alternatives to predicaments until more satisfactory long term solutions were found.

These women had in common an air of what one described as "benign certainty." They were sure of themselves, sure of their direction and attitudes. They made definite assumptions and then did not waste energy doubting, but acted confidently on them. With the creative people, their certainty was that they had to work, their artistic impulses *had* to come out. They sought to bring their own vision directly to others, because, in their views, their vision was unique and important. They had strong views of the correctness of their own judgements.

Other women with whom we spoke also had certainty about their judgements and priorities. A story editor was certain about the need to avoid total obsession with her motion picture work even if that broader perspective cost her temporary success. One lawyer was definite about not compromising her ethical standards. "I would rather be a good person than a good lawyer." All the women insisted that having children was an important priority and one which, despite all difficulties, they could incorporate into their working lives.

The certainty of these women probably facilitated their upward mobility since they were clear, definite and direct. Their strong personalities left vivid impressions. They clearly articulated points of views and did not wallow in self-doubts or second guesses. They were easy to understand. No one was bland. They were individuals. They spoke assuredly about their own competencies. They boldly identified the things at which they were good. One manager explained that her success was simply a case of "doing an outstanding job and then the cream rising to the top."

This study found that the most financially successful women rated themselves highest on self-esteem. The certainty these women expressed about their capabilities was borne out in their successes.

Confidence

Their confidence generated the same in others and it was mirrored back by the world. Gynecologist Amy Roseman was definite about her "black box" theory that predicts x + y (hard work and perseverance) will result in financially rewarding and useful work. One executive's definite priorities led her to say, "I can deal with people not liking me." One newscaster says she can let the future take care of itself because she is confident of herself as a professional. A successful doctor said women in business have to have their own hours. She clearly believes she must spend time with her children and she is willing to adjust her work schedule accordingly.

Their certainty seemed connected to their intuition. They know what they feel and have certainty they can deal with the undefined consequences of acting definitively.

Self-Control

In the long run, these women exercised strong control over their working lives and circumstances. They were activists. Their certainty allowed them to identify what they wanted. Then they attempted to design circumstances to get what they wanted. They had confidence and steadfast determination. They created and seized opportunities. For instance, two dentists adapted their practices and working schedules to accommodate their families and personal needs. Nancy Schort works four days a week in an office she established several blocks from home. One woman works only until her children get home from school. A landscape architect and a dancer established their own companies so they could set their own work schedules. All the artists work independently.

Clearly, these women wanted to choose their own directions whether they were artists, doctors or corporate managers. They did not want to be controlled, but to have control over their own futures. Often controlling behavior is thought of as masculine. But, in the past, not many women have been in positions of professional success where they might appropriately act in a controlling manner. As we expand our understanding of present day successful women, we may notice that, like successful men, successful women are also high in control. More often, in the future, control may be associated with success rather than with gender. It is also interesting that some of the control exercised by these successful women is in support of their traditional feminine roles of being wives and mothers as well as entrepreneurs.

Avoidance of Domination

A recurrent theme from these women's early recollections was the desire not to be dominated. One journalist wanted more autonomy so she would not have to get up at 4:30 in the morning—as her bosses demanded. One studio executive regretted her dependence on the clout of the big studio even while she enjoyed it. She worked briefly as an actress and discovered she did not like having to recite someone else's lines.

Risk Taking

Most of these individuals are risk takers. They are not afraid to leave secure environments for those less secure, but more in sync with their ultimate goals. One businesswoman left her happy marriage for a full year to try a job in a different city. A film producer left the secure institution of a network to freelance.

Within their careers the women with whom we spoke have shown a tendency to strike out in new directions and try new formulas.

Visibility

Visibility is another important stepping stone on the path all these women chose in order to reach their goals. Whether they were extroverts or introverts, the women found ways to be seen and noticed in their environments. They didn't spend energy on asking "Should I or shouldn't I?" They asked for what they wanted. Although one corporate executive describes her perpetual state of insecurity as feeling marooned, in business situations she temporarily overcomes her feelings of terror to say, "Look at me." She used the analogy of feeling terrified as being on a island in dense fog, but periodically the fog lifts (her terror) and she sends out little notices of visibility in the form of project proposals. "It is like little dares sent at great personal expense." Despite her fears, she is not incapacitated.

Courage

Courage is not an attribute often applied to women. Except for mothers saving their children from impending disasters, most of the tales of great courage are historically of men. If women were depicted as valorous, they were presented in the image of great helpers like Florence Nightingale. However, many of the women with whom we spoke are courageous in the traditional sense usually reserved for men. They forge ahead into uncharted waters, following their own instincts without certainty about the consequences. They are brave in trusting and trying. They are brave in creating new roles and being the heroes of success stories.

Broadness of Perspective

Despite their own disclosures as to limits, successful women display wide multiple interests which are other keys to their successes. These women exhibit, in their varied enterprises and varied tasks, an openness to gaining information, experimenting, and learning new ways of thinking and performing not only in their careers, but in many aspects of their lives.

Status Symbols

These women spoke of and displayed symbols of their accomplishments. Proudly, most women shared tales validating their accomplishments—whether that was the fact they were the first woman partner of a law firm, or the first woman pilot, had reached the top office in their corporation, or were selected by Glamour magazine as one of the top ten women in America.

In almost every woman was a lack of conceit, but still an abundance of pride and self-satisfaction in discussing her achievements.

Insecurities

Despite their vocal pride in their current achievements, many women referred to insecurities of their earlier lives that propelled them toward achievements. The significance of their descriptions of insecurities as vital factors in success is a different perspective from older studies. Women of the 1990s are crediting new components of their personalities, be they positive or negative, that are useful in moving ahead. Rather than trying to smother personality defects or insecurities, or trying to mask difficulties in their backgrounds, they point to developmental experiences that steered them in new, more positive directions. The constructive use of these experiences enabled them to become more successful.

Self-Awareness

Successful women were able to understand themselves and their work needs—power, money, attention, and social usefulness—and then arrange their lives to meet those needs. The Personality Orientation Questionnaire indicted they did spend considerable time in self reflection. They avoided self-deceit; they did not try to advance in areas for which they were not suited.

They learned for what they were willing to labor and sacrifice, and what skills they had or did not have. They created appropriate opportunities matching their interests and talents and then found meaning and satisfaction in what they had created.

CHAPTER FOUR

THE CASE OF THE MISSING MENTORS

"I signed up for exploring new frontiers."

Anna Fisher
—Astronaut

Because of the currently popular notion of the importance of mentors and role models, we were careful in our research of this group of women to remain alert for any statements they might make about people who served as models during the course of their careers.

Anna Fisher's statement was typical of the feelings expressed by the majority in this study. Surprisingly, most women did not credit any role models at all. Although women referred to people who may have inspired or helped them as they progressed, they did not feel these figures were substantially instrumental in their successes.

When asked specifically to reflect on long term role models, most of the women explicitly said they had none. They seemed to feel the type of lives they were trying to live had never been tried before and that they were like social explorers, forging their ways into new and uncharted territories without a real sense of what they might encounter along the way. No one could show them the routes because no one had been there. A movie producer, married to a fellow movie producer, articulated the dilemma: "There are no role models for what to do with the children when both my husband and I are on location."

Clearly a lot of these successful women had to create formulas that worked. Many of the women with whom Ferguson spoke implied that they were "creating" themselves and that their conduct was self-generated:

"Sometimes I feel I just hatched, because I don't feel influenced by anyone."

"I spent ten years creating me."

"As a personality, I just emerged."

"All role models have clay feet."

Subject's Role Models

Role Model	Percentage
None	43
Mother	31
Father	13
Other	13

Rejection of Role Models

The point is there were few role models, for successful 1990s women, who exemplified the way to handle the many demands placed on the contemporary professional woman who marries and has children. The pull of conscience and tradition on the one hand and new professional opportunities on the other is very conflicting. What these women are trying to do requires an unrehearsed juggling act, and those attempting this feat cannot look to older executives. Most women of the past either became career women or housewives and mothers, with distinctly different styles of behavior. There were few overlapping lifestyles at the time. The idea that a woman could successfully integrate work life and home life is a relatively new one.

Today, working women with children do not want to be bound by the limitations which confronted the women who preceded them. For younger women to pattern themselves after the few older working women, who, in turn, tell us they modeled themselves after men, would simply create a second generation male-woman. It would be as inappropriate as suggesting they pattern themselves after contemporary men. It would perpetuate the masculine stamp and ethos that remains part of the work culture and ignore the important social changes that have occurred in the last two decades.

One woman says she avoids turning male bosses into heroes: "He was clearly a superior executive, but he was also his own person. As much as I admired him, I could not look to him to dictate my way of relating to people. If I did, I would become nothing more than a clone of him. I had to find a style that worked for me, and he and all the others were going to have to learn to appreciate it."

A Previous Generation's Model Males

Hennig and Jardim, in their study, found that women born early in the century cited the significance of the models who guided them—male figures who showed them how to attain and manage success. These models, who were almost invariably fathers and bosses, were central to their accomplishments. Many of the women chose their fathers' professions, and they stayed with a single employer for most of their working years, earnestly emulating the important male figures in their lives. They patterned their own aspirations and conduct after these men. Some of them even articulated a feeling of distance from their mothers who represented traditional values they felt they had to reject in order to become successful, and relied instead on the values and examples provided by their fathers.

Women as Models for the New Generation

Women born in the mid-twentieth century have had a much wider latitude in choosing images after which to pattern their expectations. They can choose from fathers, mothers, grandparents, peers, or figures from the media. In this study, when the successful women did mention role models, significantly they responded that they looked to female figures for inspiration and guidance, and mentioned their mothers or other women much more frequently than men. Two thirds of those who cited the value of any role model at all named women: mothers, grandmothers, or other females who were their superiors.

Some of these same women confessed to having had a closer emotional relationship with the maternal figure in their family. Several described family situations in which the father was either "detached" or "emotionally remote." Again, the written questionnaire revealed that they saw greater similarities between themselves and their mothers than between themselves and their fathers. This is significant because women then take the feminine characteristics taught by their mothers into the work place. They learn poise, charm, how to dress, how to get along with a variety of people, how to be diplomatic, and other social behaviors and attitudes from their mothers.

Social Behavior

Several successful women perceived their homemaker mothers as exemplary individuals, active in the community and socially energetic. In one case, a producer recalled her mother had been a frustrated housewife, but, even so, she was a strong presence. "She was bossy—a real decision maker. Her power was apparent in her relationships with her friends and in neighborhood dynamics. In addition, she ran the family."

Acceptability of Working

The assumption that was implicit in the way this group of women was reared was that it was acceptable for women to work outside the house. More than half the women had mothers who had jobs at some point in their lives, and several had mothers who returned to school for training in later life. Mothers who never worked outside the home were also influential, but one-third of the subjects recalled the lack of satisfaction that permeated these lives of exclusive domesticity. Often, these mothers expressed regrets over careers forsaken and opportunities missed.

These attitudes within the family are more than peripherally interesting. The importance of a mother's attitude in shaping her daughter's professional aspirations has been confirmed by studies indicating that the daughters of working women score noticeably higher on career orientation tests. It is also true that when girls sense their mothers are wholly satisfied with domesticity, they are more likely to choose that life for themselves. Conversely, a mother's dissatisfaction at home has a way of infusing a daughter with a greater sense of career ambition. Women with mothers who worked generally have higher job skills themselves, and more challenging positions than women whose mothers remained at home.

For instance, dentist Nancy Schort remembers her mother going out and getting a job as a medical technician when Nancy and her brother were youngsters. She saw, first-hand, a woman responding to both the needs of her family and the requirements of a job. More importantly, she remembers her mother's excitement and general sense of pride; no sooner had she gone out and obtained a job than she began to lose weight and to make new friends. In a few words, she was happier.

The behavior these daughters imitated was based on a close view of family-oriented women working happily outside the home. Daughters learned the attitude that it is rewarding for women to work and have families.

Most of the women whose mothers worked did not simply go out and imitate their maternal examples. They chose different fields of endeavor at different levels. Whereas the mothers had taken jobs as nurses, bookkeepers, secretaries, medical technicians or as their husbands' assistants, the daughters pursued more elevated professional callings. What the working mothers provided was a sense of the importance and the excitement of being productive in the outside world.

Even the mothers who didn't work expressed happi

ness with their daughters' accomplishments. Many of the successful women talked about the vicarious pleasure their mothers experienced, and the fact that this parental enthusiasm represented an implicit endorsement of the lives they had chosen. In some ways, the role modeling worked in reverse.

Independence and Inspiration

Another important attitude these women absorbed from their mothers was a need for independence. A physician said she had gotten the message from her mother starting at a very early age. "You are your own person. Don't ever be overly dependent on a man." Another white collar professional said her mother instilled her with the sense that a woman could do anything.

On the other hand, Cherilyn Sheets, a Newport Beach dentist, has exercised her own sense of independence and is happily married to a man who for a long period of time was earning about one-third her salary. He deliberately chose a job that allowed him the flexibility to go on trips with her. Cherilyn says she took a lesson from her mother. "Although she was happy as a housewife, she encouraged me to be financially independent."

One manager describes her Asian mother as someone who deviated from her traditional culture in that she was both unconventional and firm. Her daughter was impressed with the fact that it was possible to violate your cultural traditions.

Creating New Models

When interviewing astronaut Anna Fisher, she had just returned from a year's maternity leave with her second child and was two months into a self-negotiated, part-time status with NASA. She was not sure how the negotiations would proceed or of the eventual impact on her career. She is admired for paving the way and being bold in creating a new work pattern. We laughed as she said: "It isn't exactly what I had in mind when I signed up for *exploring new frontiers.*"

Anna has made one flight into space between the births of her six year old and one year old daughters. "On a technical level, I feel I have demonstrated that I can compete with men. I take my job as a parent seriously and don't feel comfortable handing over the job of raising my children to others. But with two children I'm finding it hard to do both. I don't see men putting that kind of effort into kids . . . the same as women do.

"I enjoy being a parent. It is so much fun and so rewarding. I would like another child, but I'd like some spacing so I would have time to give."

Her decision to have—or not have—a third child later appeared to be related to her work concerns and the total time it takes. "In the professional setting, I am constantly trying to juggle the two roles. Either I am not happy or my job suffers."

She has felt the impact of her children on her career. She received her crew assignment to fly (into space) two weeks before she delivered her first child. There was no question as to whether she would accept the assignment. This was a path she had been on for years. It was just fate that these two paths were climaxing at the same time. Anna never really took any maternity leave with her first child. Her daughter was born July 29th and she returned almost immediately to work. In October she was assigned to be a CapCon (capsule communicator). She didn't want to give up that experience, but she was also breast feeding at the same time and managed both jobs.

"At that time, work was number one and my daughter was also number one. They were equal priorities which I juggled on a daily basis. I don't think Kristin was hurt. The thing I am finding out now is that they care less at that age. It isn't as hard on a small child as long as there is a good, loving "backup Mom." I took my flight into space when Kristin was fifteen months old. I knew what the risks were, and I knew that a disaster was possible. Maybe I valued my time with Kristin even more. I was concerned because, as her mother, I know I am irreplaceable. However, I didn't waste a lot of time on that thought since I was on a path that was set. My mother was very helpful and made all the difference. She came to stay six weeks before my flight and stayed on for a few weeks after.

"After the flight I was assigned to another crew. This was just before the *Challenger* accident. But I was feeling, at that time, I wanted more time with Kristin.

"For my colleagues, work is always number one. There is the assumption that in order to do your job well you have to be available to travel on a moment's notice. If the weather is bad, the better answer is to stay overnight rather than push it. I'm not a pilot, so that is not my decision, but I might have a different orientation wanting to get back to my family. Juggling a demanding career and a family is tough.

"I have fewer answers than when I was starting out. Then, I thought you just get a lot of great help and go on. Now, I have two wonderful daughters who really thrive when I give them attention. I think they are too young to be farming them out to car pools. If I watch my older daughter's ballet class, I might see an interaction where her feelings get hurt—where a mother makes a difference.

"There are twelve other women in my office, four with children."

She reflected on the best time to have children.

"I couldn't possibly have done this in medical school. There is something to making your initial space flight first so you can prove yourself. You are then a proven commodity."

As to a choice if she had to make one between parenting and her career: "I love my career. I love flying in space and I love my children. It's difficult.

"What I wish is that there were a phase where you have your children and raise them and still keep your foot in the door. The problem is that I'm not talking about two or three years. If you have three children, it means six to ten years. I would have to continue doing what I am doing now without being in flight status for five to ten years."

But she quotes from Kristin's favorite movie, *The Little Mermaid*: "Life is full of tough choices." She is quite aware that if she took that much time off, she would be in her late forties or fifties: "Your useful career life to NASA lessens at fifty. Some astronauts have flown after that, but not many. If we lived in an ideal world, I would work part-time for five to ten years and then resume my full-time career."

If she were full-time, she would have to do T-38 flying to stay current ("I am not a pilot, so it is important to keep up with issues of flying"), spend time in simulators, make personal appearances and work particular jobs. At present, she is doing only one thing—working on the space station. She still goes to meetings and stays current, but does no personal appearances and is not doing T-38 flying.

According to Anna, it is too soon to tell whether the cutback has harmed her. "If I did come back full-time after this year and worked diligently for about twelve to eighteen months, I would probably be assigned to a flight, but the choices I have made raise questions in people's minds about my competency and dedication. Space exploration is a hard business to leave. I think if it were anything else, I would leave and then try to come back after my children were older. Interestingly, I don't see any of my male colleagues feeling the same conflicting choices."

Her husband, whom she married when she was twenty-eight, is also a doctor and an astronaut. For a short time he gave up his medical practice while learning to be an astronaut, but he now works full-time at NASA and also one day and two nights of twelve-hour shifts at a medical emergency clinic. When his wife has to be at work at 8:00 a.m., he takes their daughter to school. "When I have to be at work by eight o'clock, I have to get up at 4:00 a.m. to get it all done and spend some time with my children before I leave. At some point, if I were exhausted all the time and not having fun, I could say, 'Well, Kristin, I could cut back on some of your activities and make my career the #1 priority.' My husband feels strongly about maintaining his medical skills and being able to take care of the family. It is difficult. He feels if he stepped away from his medical group, the opportunity wouldn't come back.

"I feel strongly about my responsibility as a mother, but space flight is great, the space station is great. I brought Kristin's first grade class for a visit and seeing it through their eyes was even more exciting. I think space exploration is the next major chapter in mankind's history. I am proud of my small part in that history.

"I view this as a special time period of life. This is a useful role to society."

She has been helped by two male pilots, both of whom are particularly family-oriented. "One told me he thinks what I'm doing is the right decision. Those two guys and friends made me feel much better about my decision. One even went to bat for me with my management and probably helped the decision to work part-time for a year turn out favorably."

When asked how she had succeeded, Fisher said: "No member of my family ever went to college before. My mom is from Europe and my father joined the military before he graduated from high school. He retired and worked in the warehouse at MacDonald Douglas. He died early, at fifty-seven. From my earliest memory, I wanted to go to college and have a profession. But my mother never pushed me. I have three younger brothers. We're all close, but really different. I always did well in school and got reinforcement from the teachers. Since I was shy, I would never have considered theater arts. But I was great in science and math and got that reinforcement."

Her major tip: "If you're going to have both a family and career, choose a field in which you have some control over your life."

Two Different Female Models

A clear case of someone acquiring certain attributes based on an example set at home was illustrated by a law school graduate, Jane H.. Over the years, she demonstrated her capacity for the law, first at Harvard University Law School, and, eventually, within a major metropolitan law firm in which she became the first female partner. She loves her job, but also loves her domestic life and talks about "moonlighting" as a housewife in a manner that indicates her enjoyment in her husband, cooking and gardening.

She thinks she acquired her taste for these two contrasting worlds from the two female figures closest to her, her mother and her grandmother.

Her mother was a secretary who worked her way into an executive position. As a child, Jane had many opportunities to observe her mother's professional side, and remembers her as being extremely effective with people. She became Jane's image because the daughter could see that she worked hard and developed a respect for her ambition.

On the other hand, Jane feels that she was nurtured by her mother's mother, who lived with the family and was "the domestic one," cooking and cleaning. She was the person who listened when Jane felt hurt or neglected. "Grandma had a soft touch. If we did something wrong, Grandma got us out of it." She also demonstrated the pleasures to be derived from domesticity.

Values

Another corporate executive states that she, too, learned much from her grandparents, who, like her parents, were both college educated. Her grandfather, especially, emphasized the importance of getting an education, even though he was a farmer. He financed his grandchildren's educations by taking loans on his land.

Her mother was also an inspiration. She remembers

being sent to the neighborhood store and coming back with the groceries, but, because she was black, they would not give her a bag. "I'd come out of the store and my mother would make me go back and get a bag. She taught me a valuable lesson which is still part of my philosophy: Always ask—all they can do is say no." In her experience, more people are inclined to say "yes."

One airline pilot, Lynn Ripplemeyer, remembers a significant difference between her mother's and her father's outlook on life. She says it was her mother's values that set the predominate guidelines for her own life and feels it was her mother's attitude that provided a foundation for her to be able to buck tradition and become one of the first female pilots.

Her father was German; his attitude was, "People make rules because they know more than you and, therefore, you should follow them." By contrast, her mother felt that "Rules are made for the benefit of the majority. You decide if the situation fits you and abide accordingly."

The difference in outlook was crystalized in an incident from her youth she considered formative. Her family was a religious family. "We grew up going to church every Sunday and never really argued with the idea of God. But the notion of this church telling me what to do all the time didn't set right, and I got involved in studying other religions. It gave me other ways to think about life."

The first rule she broke was deciding that reincarnation was a definite possibility. Two-thirds of the world believed in the phenomenon, and, she thought, "Who are we to say it doesn't make sense?" She remembers giving a speech on reincarnation in front of her minister, who was also the speech teacher. He told her if she persisted in her belief, she couldn't continue as a member of the church and take communion. "Fine," she stated, "if the church won't let me think the way I want, I won't be part of it." So, at age fifteen, she stopped going to services.

Instead, every Sunday, she would go riding on her horse in "God's country," and have her own communion with nature and her thoughts. The reactions of her parents were true to form. "Mom thought it was fine," she remembers, but her father didn't. He thought her actions represented a rebellion against rules made for the good of the group. She encountered the same situation later when she challenged the rules regarding how men and women are supposed to act—who could or couldn't fly an airplane. She vowed that, like her mother, she would only play by the rules that made sense for her.

Despite this, however, she still learned useful lessons from her father. "Work was my father's life," she says, "He was a rancher and enjoyed what he did. He didn't take vacations because, for him, there was nothing else to do. I saw him be his own boss, make decisions, take risks, and live with the consequences. His income varied widely, but I never remember his complaining. He took it all in stride. We all shared, for the good of the family, and our lifestyle was all by our own efforts."

The head of a hospital claimed that one key to her success was making decisions on the basis of what she had learned from her mother. She remembers her as a very religious person and, consequently, quite fatalistic. She instructed her daughter that no matter what happened, things work out for the best. As a result, she learned early in life to try hard, but to avoid blaming herself in the event of failure, because, if something didn't come to pass, it was logically not meant to be. To her, there was no such thing as a wrong road taken or a foolish choice. It was this outlook on life that she feels has made it easier for her to think clearly and act decisively, because she was taught never to be fearful of the consequences.

Sources of Confidence

Gynecologist Amy Roseman was the only female among nine grandchildren. Consequently, she was her grandmother's "shining star." Her grandmother was a strong-minded lady who had graduated from Barnard College—against great odds—and had become a teacher. She encouraged her granddaughter to pursue whatever course she wanted, regardless of the fact she was female. She instilled her with confidence, telling Amy that some day she would be somebody.

With this foundation, Amy found other female role models as she matured. Her mother went back to school while Amy was still a teenager, eventually earning a degree. A female doctor at the research center where she was employed provided Amy with inspiration to apply to medical school. Once enrolled, a woman ahead of her became such an inspiration that Roseman later joined her as a partner. "When I asked her if I was doing something right, she always assured me of my own judgment." Both these women, like her grandmother, reinforced her sense of herself.

Other Sources of Inspiration

There were a number of other figures this group of successful women admired: male friends, husbands, fathers, media heroines and leaders from the Women's Movement. These women consistently compared themselves to the people around them. For example, if friends were applying to law school, they'd think, "Why not me?" A black federal district court judge says that, when she was young, she found role models among the lawyers, like Thurgood Marshall, who were active in the Civil Rights Movement. Observing them provided her with the inspiration to do her own good works.

Using Images to Develop Personal Standards

One businesswoman with whom we spoke came from a working class background. Her father was a policeman, while her mother grew up poor and uneducated in rural Kentucky. While studying at a large southern university, she felt there were no successful people in her family to serve as an example, and volunteered to act as director of a speakers' program so that she could invite successful people to campus and "gather their secrets." These people were heroes to her, and she made a great effort to study their thinking in the course of acting as hostess.

What she learned from this experience, however, was that successful people didn't necessarily fit the bill as role models. As she discovered, "they weren't always big people, but just little people who had been put into positions of being big. I learned that many of them were simply poor little guys with money, bullheadedness, or luck."

She had expected them to be giants. Instead, their very ordinariness boosted her own confidence. She found it was the same when she entered the working world. Even the big-time import-export operator who eventually gave her a break and made her a millionaire before she was thirty, was no idol. She thought of him more as a "plodder" than a risk-taker. His attitude was, no matter what happened, he was just going to sell his goods. Consequently, she denies having any role models and feels her style "just emerged."

A television producer built her confidence while working as a secretary for a writer. As she watched him struggling, she cast aside her old notion that a writer *knew*, from birth, what his or her destiny was. Suddenly she felt confident about her own writing. His ordeal has served as an inspiration.

Susan C., an entrepreneur, provides a good example of someone who developed her own standards—with the careful consideration of would-be role models. Her motto is "Whatever you don't know, turn to experience. I was brought up around adults. By listening to them you can gain two lifetime experiences for the price of one. When my grandfather would say, 'I tried this and it didn't work,' I listened. I figured if it didn't work for him I won't do it. Tradition is important, but I don't consider it a given. I just consider it input." Consequently, she feels safe and secure. Her orientation is to enjoy and test the world. "I don't see limits. I have no fear except snakes."

Although these successful women denied, for the most part, that their idols were male, and deemphasized the importance of the effect their fathers had on them, more than two thirds had fathers who were very successful. Certainly this partially explains how the "habit" of success could have been incorporated into their own future behavior. They could observe the personification of ambition, drive and social grace in their own milieu.

Another paradox in their thinking occurred on their written questionnaires, where they indicated influential mentors at some points in their careers. Yet, most still felt that they were "self-made" women.

Perhaps the significance of this is best seen in their *explicit* denial of role models. Clearly, they observed successful people and even singled out individuals for guidance. It seemed obvious they had people to teach them, but, when they were questioned directly about whether they had role models, they said no, since they were, for the most part, women playing roles that they had created for themselves.

These women have addressed the problem of not having role models by creating new standards, by assembling a kind of composite picture to replace the missing role model portrait. They observed their feminine mothers, and their masculine fathers, plus the people they met on their paths, and they compiled a new picture of success.

A news anchorwoman crystallizes the modern feeling on role models: "I only had role models in the sense of picking out characteristics from different people and observing them to extract what did and didn't work."

There emerged two key findings in this study. Most women say they had no role models for what they do, because they are, for the most part, the very first women holding that specific position of power. They are setting the standard, creating themselves, acting as pioneers.

When they were asked about people they admired in their lives, many cited females, not males (as in the earlier Hennig-Jardim study). They pieced together archetypes from mothers, grandmothers, celebrities. Forty percent had working mothers, modeling femininity, at work.

They learned some things from a wide variety of other sources, such as fathers and other men in their lives: relatives, male friends, mates. But the implication is, because most of these women had strong mothers—women (many college educated) who preceded them and worked— they had more feminine than masculine images for professional success.

CHAPTER FIVE

SUPPORTING PLAYERS FROM THE HOMEFRONT

"My husband, as time went on, was increasingly involved in the rearing of the kids and he has grown along with me."

Madeleine Kunin
—Governor of Vermont

The picture painted in current cultural stereotypes often portrays the successful woman as someone who has a fabulous career, but comes home and cries alone in an empty house. A common assumption is that most accomplished career women are single. However, this picture of loneliness at the top was not supported by the testimony of the married women with children in this study. They saw their relationships with husbands and children not as incidental, but rather instrumental, in their successes.

The support provided took many forms. It ranged from simple and unconditional love to intense collaborative business planning and strategizing. It came in different forms from different mates, whether these spouses were younger, older, richer, poorer, more successful, or perhaps less so. Additional support came from other sources: family, friends, household help, movements, associations, and, significantly, other women.

This also represented a change from the experience of previous generations of successful women. According to earlier research, most married working women had limited sources of support, and they felt much more that their struggles were exclusively their own. Their supporters, when they existed, had invariably been men in paternal roles: fathers, bosses, and, occasionally in later life, older mates. They specifically denied any support from other women, and felt cut off from their biological peers. Perhaps this partially explains their exaggerated independence. They were "pioneers" on the frontier of a movement, traveling to a new land without the companionship of like-minded allies.

However, the women we interviewed felt they had many more sources of help, and had more latitude in choosing partners who would compliment them. Society had allowed these women to pursue top professional positions, and they felt free to choose (or not choose) partners who endorsed that goal. They also felt a woman could pursue a career in tandem with her husband, or perhaps choose a limited career and rely on the literal "support" of a mate, if that suited her. It became obvious that they felt they were beneficiaries of the public's increasing acceptance of a diversity of lifestyles. Indeed, many expressed the thought that the same choice of flexibility was now available to men as well.

Many responded the proof that society has changed often comes in small bits of evidence such as the realization that many of their friends are having their first children in their thirties. It's a morale booster to realize that there are many other women who also desire families and home lives which validate their own decisions.

These women said the supporting relationships in their lives had provided them with peace of mind, stimulation, confirmation, and opportunity. The two most important forms of support they listed were emotional love and endorsement of their chosen roles.

Nancy Evans, former head of Doubleday, feels the support of a mate is paramount: "The best thing a woman can do is marry a good guy."

Spousal Support

Nature of Support Received	% of Women
Emotional Security	31%
Endorsement of Professional Role	24%
Providing Skills	17%
Providing Counsel	14%
Providing Assistance	10%
Financial Support	3%

Supreme Court Justice Sandra Day O'Connor contributes her own story.

"I continued working full time when I had my first child. We had a very good baby sitter. The baby sitter left at the same time the second child came and it was not possible to continue. I stayed home and tried to locate household help so I would have some flexibility of action.

"I used that time to do voluntary activities in the community related to my interests and concerns." Finally, the judge found she was stretched thin with volunteer work. "It was hard to say 'no' to worthy things. I needed to bring some order into my life. I did want to keep a hand in the legal profession. I would have preferred part time work, but there wasn't any. I wasn't sure employment of any kind would be available. After a number of years, I finally persuaded the state to let me work part time. But it was very hard, and I never had enough time. It was sometimes a struggle to keep up with the household and attend to the children's needs. The weekend went by so fast with all the errands and things that must be done.

"I remember the biggest problems with our children were vacations and summers. In their free time I didn't want the kids at home alone watching television; so I tried to devise ways to avoid that. As they got older, I tried to interest my youngest son in music and so time was taken up with lessons and band. The eldest son was very interested in swimming, and that took care of all of his time. The middle son was a mountain climber.

"We tried to make use of teenaged youngsters who could drive the boys to appointments and play with them, and who were good role models. The teenagers wanted the extra money, and they enjoyed teaching our boys to throw balls, ice skate and swim."

When asked if it was difficult to find good child care, O'Connor said, "I spent a lot of energy on finding good people to care for the children. I occasionally found male caretakers through friends, or people I knew and could make judgments about.

"We had one very special man whose wife had done housework and he did gardening. He came to our house, not as a sitter, but more like a companion. He was in his seventies and he was like a grandfather. Many times, I recall Brian—our middle boy—sitting on his lap when I got home and this man was reading stories. I tried to reach out to people who were compassionate and available.

"I was lucky, because I grew up on a ranch and my parents and brother were still there; so we would take the boys to the ranch every summer.

"We tried to schedule all the vacations with the boys doing family activities like camping, hiking, skiing. And we had a really good time together.

"I am pleased the boys seemed to be developing into responsible men. I didn't want them to suffer. Oh, they might have needed new shoes or clothing, and I didn't have as much time, but I didn't have as much time for those things for myself either.

"The good side is that they are very sensible and independent. For example, our dog was hit by a car when no adult was there and they did the sensible thing. They found an old door and made it into a stretcher and carried the dog to the vet. I was proud of that. Another time a swarm of bees got under the siding of the house . . . and a queen bee can cause a disaster. The boys had the presence of mind to look in the yellow pages and call a bee keeper. That was most impressive."

When asked about her husband's role, she said, "He had no great interest in changing diapers, but he was a great companion for the children, particularly as they got older," she replied. "He never complained about my working. He was just terrific. He moved to Washington, D.C. with me." He was very encouraging when O'Connor was appointed to the Supreme Court.

"Sure, there is guilt. I was at work one day when one of the boys had a fall and hurt his head rather badly. He had to go with one of my neighbors to the hospital. Of course, there are times when something like that happens, but we do the best we can, and I was never one to look back and agonize.

"For women in the nineties, the number one priority is child care. We have to solve it in the best way we can, sometimes with family members, sometimes with others. We can muddle through, but there is comfort seeking quality advice from professionals from women's institutions and associations where there are other women dealing with the same issues and problems.

"Employers can look at the possibilities of child care on the premises. They can consider flexible time and part time when women need it."

O'Connor feels that taking time off didn't ultimately hamper her career, but "I worried when I took those years that I would lose my skills, and I would not be marketable.

"One help is that nowadays women live longer. We spend more years in employment and really have time for a couple of careers. If a few years are taken out, all is not lost."

When asked about the things that contributed to her success, she said, "Growing up on a ranch, I learned about independence and *taking care of my own needs*. Since there wasn't any school within thirty-five miles, I had to leave my parents' ranch and live with my grandmother. I was terribly homesick all the time. But my grandmother was extremely devoted to me. She kept telling me I could do anything I wanted to do. She was always supportive. She and my parents were never negative. They didn't tell me where to apply to school or law school. They were always thrilled for me to be progressing in school. My mother had gone to college. My father didn't get to go. I have one brother and one sister, ten and eleven years younger.

"Women need flexibility. Women are able to handle multiple roles. I am constantly impressed. Women are a lot stronger than we think."

What did she see as her biggest problems or disadvantages? "I was probably more apt to tell my children what I thought they ought to do. Maybe that was an outgrowth or result of my being a judge or legislator. I've done that a long time and it is hard to turn it off. My comments weren't always welcome. But I was so concerned about not having the children drift around when they were not in school, it was an easier role for me to step in and plan their time."

As to whether she felt working full time was detrimental to her children, since she had already mentioned it voluntarily as a concern, she said, "You'd have to ask them. It may have been, but, of course, I think they are wonderful young men." Asked if there were impacts on her marriage from the demands of her career, she answered, "No, it's much more uncertain with child rearing."

KINDS OF SUPPORT

Unconditional Love

Most of the successful women with whom we spoke were content with a simple form of support: unconditional love. Comfort was derived from a husband who, as one professional woman said, "loved me whether or not I was a good lawyer."

Professional Endorsement from Mates

The support that meant a great deal to these women, second in importance only to unconditional love, was the sense that their mates endorsed their professional aspirations. This was not limited to the idea of sharing domestic responsibilities or dividing up the housework and child care, but rather the sense that the man in a woman's life shared her vision and truly wished her to realize her potential. Not only did many of these women have spouses who never tried to dissuade them from working, but a great many of their mates simply assumed, without question, that they should have a professional life.

Dentist Nancy Schort had the backing of her husband when she made her decision to enter dental school at age twenty-six. She had bemoaned the fact that if she started her training so late in life, she would be thirty by the time she graduated and started her practice. His matter of fact response was, "How old will you be if you don't go?" He also graciously sacrificed an influential position with his bank in Europe to accommodate her goal.

Surgeon Marjorie Fine had both a husband and two small children when she enrolled in medical school. Her husband was the "in residence" parent when she was working. During her training, she says, "I slept in the hospital every other night."

Some of the women described their husbands as the primary nurturers of the children. Sharon Flaherty said her secret weapon is that her husband is a full time dad. She has the support of having someone care for the children who loves them as much as she does. Dr. Amy Roseman expressed similar sentiments, saying she was grateful to her husband for his nurturing of their children.

There are incredible stories of both the encouragement of husbands and the sharing of tasks. At least twenty percent of the husbands had to live apart from their spouses for periods of time and were still supportive, like Sandra Day O'Connor's husband, who moved to follow his wife's career.

Marcy Carsey was clear and conscious about her ambitions. There was never any question that she wanted a high powered career and her husband has been supportive all along the way. Barbara Boxer's husband was originally asked to run for the office she eventually sought. He did not want to give up his law practice and encouraged her to campaign, saying, "Someone in the family has to represent the issues."

Geraldine Ferraro's husband helped with the dishes and babies. "He needed less sleep than I did; so he would get up in the night when the kids cried." Marcy Tiffany is very close to her husband. There is no judgment decision about either of their careers in which the other is not involved. One executive feels support—as part of a dual career couple—is knowing her husband could take physical care of the family.

Advice and Counsel

Many of the women talked about husbands with whom they could discuss all the ups and downs of career-life. Cherilyn Sheets practiced her professional presentations on her husband. He watched her slide shows and her preparations, providing early critiques. He even arranged his work life in order to be there for his wife.

Balance

Many of the women felt supported by people in their lives who helped them achieve a form of balance. One contributed the opinion that her husband is more relaxed and easy going than she is. She feels he has a calming influence on her and provides a reassuring perspective on things when family demands and work responsibilities conflict. A producer/director, who is very deep and intense, feels complimented by her husband who is more outgoing and light-hearted. A business executive thinks she is a good idea person. She originated the concept for her children's boutique, but her husband accompanied her to the bank and helped negotiate the loans necessary to launch the business. Nancy Schort was advised by her banker-husband when she graduated from dental school and needed help setting up a practice.

Rebecca Sinkler is the Editor-in-Chief of *The New York Times Book Review* and her story of working to attain a balance in her home life, while moving ahead, is a significant statement on how successful married women with children have had to create new patterns of family life with no precedents.

Married at twenty, having had two years of college, she completed one more year and then "had babies." She stayed home—with no help—until her youngest child was a few years old, then she went back to the University of Pennsylvania, juggling family and school.

She was an oddity. As a woman coming back to school with three children, she remembers being discouraged from participation in the Honors Program by a grumpy professor of 18th century English literature, a "horrible old guy." Prior to recommending her for honors, he first asked if she had help at home and, when he found out she didn't, said he couldn't recommend her.

"There were quite a lot of raised eyebrows about women with kids going back to school. I was one of the first, but I got a lot of support, too. What drove me was that, finally, I got bored doing housework. And suddenly I saw I was extremely over-involved psychologically in my first child's success. I can remember sitting at his swim lessons and getting ulcers wanting him to be the best. And my daughter had a very different personality than mine; she *didn't* do so well in school, but was very creative. I felt I was getting overly involved in them and that it wasn't healthy.

"I wrote down a five-year plan that had to do with teaching. I actually tried it and found I hated teaching and so I thought I better do what I really wanted to do, way back, which was to write. I got a job doing local journalism —reporting on sewers and township meetings. That educated me about the community, as well as about my career.

"Starting when I was thirty-nine, I interned at a small start-up city newspaper, and thirty-nine was really old to begin a career in journalism. But it was the best thing I ever did. With my first job, I was shaking in my shoes in awe of journalism and in awe of the younger people and their expertise. But this will show you one advantage of age. I remember reporting for work, and there wasn't enough furniture, just a rickety old chair and a typewriter. I was given some list to type. The boss, who was younger than I, stuck his head in my door and said he wanted the typewriter I was using. I said I would give it to him when I was finished, which, of course, was correct. A few days later, he stuck his head back in and told me he couldn't believe that an intern would have the presence to defy him.

"But, at thirty-nine, I had already brought up three children—and taken care of groups of kids and learned a lot about human relationships. I still have situations at work that I handle in ways I deal with my kids. Having children makes you think about people and things instead of machines." When she went back to work full time her kids were fifteen, thirteen and nine.

The newspaper folded, but Rebecca made good contacts.

"I was so green I hadn't realized how useful my skills were. But people told me I could freelance, which I did until I was hired by *The Philadelphia Inquirer.* Still I had to work very hard. I basically started as a secretary and I had to keep asking for more." After her internship, she was doing freelance work and working for *The Inquirer,* when the secretary quit. They offered her that job at the exact same time her kids had just started summer camp. She said, "sure," and, within a month, had figured out how not to type and worked like a dog when they asked if she thought she would like to try editing. Once she stayed up at night with a thirty-page story spread out all over the bedroom and loved the challenge.

It took two years for her to get ahead at the paper. "The top boss kept saying, 'Nobody comes in as a secretary and ends up as an editor.' " But her immediate boss fought for her and she never let up. "I don't know how he stood me. Month after month, I would ask him, 'When am I going to get paid for what I am actually doing?' and 'When am I going to get a title?' My immediate boss made it a fulltime project to keep me away from the top boss, but he did counsel me. He taught me to edit, and, from him, I also learned to behave with a certain protocol in a corporate setting.

"All the time I was nudging, I continued to do the work. That—and luck—is the way I got ahead. I really do feel there is something to being in the right place at the right time. Affirmative Action also impressed on men the need to find competent women, and the women's movement was helpful. In addition, I was smart and worked hard.

"During my schooling, my husband was tremendously supportive but, when I went to work, I was obsessed and it wasn't too pleasant. We still had this big house in the suburbs with this big lawn and yard. We even went through some very bad periods. It was hard on my husband, because I got so consumed in work, I was not showing him any attention. The marriage almost fell apart. But what helped was excellent therapy. It was built on understanding. We began to listen to each other. We could get the painful things out.

"A lot of our marriage was about *power* and I was gaining power at an enormous rate. The therapy gave us the protection to fight fairly. No matter how awful we had been to one another during the week, we would know there was someone else who would be there at the end of the week to mediate and help us resolve what seemed to be unresolvable conflicts. As a young married woman, I had not been very able to *ask for things* for myself, and therapy helped me make demands. But, all this while, I was clear that I didn't want my marriage to fall apart and, luckily, neither did my husband. We worked through the chaos and built a stronger foundation.

"We also made a lot of compromises. David is an independent investment adviser. We moved from a big house in the suburbs, with lawns he loved, to the city to make it easier for me, but I commute to New York every day, because he has such a good business in Philadelphia. It takes about an hour and a half—total three hours a day— but it is good work time. Still, it is tiring. David doesn't want me to spend the night in New York. I would like nothing better than to get a room about once a week, but, psychologically, it is important to him to have me home. Also, there is a lot of socializing and parties in this business— such as meeting authors and publishers—that take place in the evening. But I have managed to do this at lunch, and, after four or five years, people know this. Now, it doesn't bother David to have such a high-visability wife—in fact, he revels in it. He is very centered.

"Life at home is more leisurely now that our children are grown, but, during our active parenting period, I had to work exceptionally hard to move ahead. My husband ended up doing all the week night cooking and laundry. He agreed, mainly because I wasn't there to do it. He could either have waited for me to get home late to start cooking, or do it himself. And he was well brought up. He was not spoiled by his mother. She was hard on him and made him cook and work in the garden. He was made to do a lot of chores for which she never apologized, so, consequently, he never expected to be waited on.

"Our family had a *great* moment in feminist history when, one day, my fourteen-year-old son, Henry, turned to David and said, 'Gee, Dad, what were some of your Dad's favorite recipes?'

"When Henry was in his teens, he was a happy kid, but a terrible student. He had a million friends, but would not do his homework. As a junior in high school, he called a meeting of his teachers and parents to inform us he was dropping out of school. He did this in November and looked for a job, but returned by January." Sinkler didn't try to prevent this; Henry had been so unmotivated that she took this as a positive attempt to take control of his life.

When asked how this impacted her feelings as a mother, she replied, "I constantly knew I was a bad mother and had guilt about spending time away from the kids. But I also knew, on an emotional level, that I was a good mother. I adored the kids and was with them from very early on. I knew the die was already cast when I returned to work. All in all, our children had it pretty good. I love the statement of D.W. Winncott about the 'good enough' mother. You just have to be good enough; that gives you broad latitude."

In recent years, her oldest son, Wharton, majored in history at Princeton, but decided he wanted to be a scientist and is now at the University of Pennsylvania. "And he will be a very good one," Sinkler boasts. Interestingly, her daughter is now a full time mother with a year old child. She has been offered two or three jobs in her field of public radio, but turned them down. "My feelings about that are ambivalent. I admire her; at that age I felt that my first job would be my only chance. But she is the type that always wanted to have children—she always babysat, etcetera—and she says it is just for two or three years. Maybe, in the back of her mind is the model of her mother—me. When I went back to work, I *definitely* felt the kids were already secure, and that combined with my feeling that I was overly involved in my oldest son to almost a harmful degree. The youngest is at least as well adjusted as the others, and he is the product of more shared parenting than the others."

She offers these tips to women in the workplace. "Fight hard for what you need and for support. You can redo priorities. You can go to another city or the suburbs and give up the fancy life: you don't have to have expensive vacations, but be mindful of sacrificing the pleasures of your children."

She went on, "Family issues should be high on the national agenda. Everyone should be thinking about them: abortion and good day care. Our nation has always been chintzy and cheap about children, and it is terrible.

"My wish is that everyone had the privilege I've had, which is to be with their kids and have meaningful work."

Partners in the Same Field

Interestingly, some of the most successful women in this study have mates who are in the same field. Assuming that their original choices of life partners were not just a matter of being too busy to meet men involved in different careers, they reap the rewards of having a companion who understands their trials and tribulations. The comradeship generated from this shared perspective and mutual understanding is both a personal and professional plus.

One portfolio manager takes great pleasure in the intellectual pleasure her husband provides. "When you are an economist," she says, "it's simply more fun if you're riding the subway together every morning talking about discount rates and the federal deficit."

Ellen Gordon, the President of Tootsie Roll, was one of the first women to head a corporation listed on the New York Stock Exchange. Throughout her career, she has had the support of both her father, who founded the business, and her husband, who was the corporation's chief operating officer. Even though her husband was involved in another business of his own in another city, he endorsed her extensive travel schedule because it was in their common interest.

Mutual Support

Julia Thomas has one grown child and is an equal partner in an architectural firm with the man who provided her first break in the profession eleven years ago— her husband. She now serves as the Chairman of the Board of Bobrow/Thomas associates, a Los Angeles-based architecture, planning and consulting firm. Together, they manage a staff of one hundred whose specialty is designing hospitals and other large institutional buildings. The partners' offices in West Los Angeles give an immediate impression of creative activity and energy. Thomas is a vital and upbeat female. "I'm the kind of person who feels that if there is a $100 million project to take on, I'm the one to do it—and I should." She adds, "I think big."

Julia also found time to serve as president of The Committee of 200, a select group of top women entrepreneurs and high level managers.

Julia was the youngest of three girls and consequently "spoiled." She says, "I never had boyfriends. I put up barriers and focused on other things. I never really intended to marry, but just fell into it at twenty-five." For nine years she was married to a man her own age. Then, after they divorced, she returned to U.C.L.A. to study architecture and got her first job at William Pereira Associates by responding to a classified advertisement.

Thomas' confidence in her professional abilities and her focus on good work comes, she says, from her grandfather, whose Puritan sensibility dictated that he subjugate his emotional life to his work. However, Julia's current success is partly due to the influence of her architect-husband, Michael, who had the ability to spot her talent before they were married. She was a student in one of his classes, and he was drawn to her intelligence, good judgment, and "incredible beauty."

They were ideally suited as partners. He is respectful and supportive of her, and she values his ability and "extraordinary taste." She says, "Clients want to see us both. I perform the conceptual role, and act as the generalist. I like to bring people together and bring out the best in them. But I am not a good detail person. My managerial weakness is cost saving. Michael is better at those things."

Julia is aware her good looks are conspicuous, but does not capitalize on flirtatiousness or old-fashioned feminine wiles. She shakes hands, and conducts herself in a low-key manner. "It's effective," she says, "because once you are talking about an idea, it is the idea and no longer the personality that is important."

Julia has confidence in her partner, and, above all, trusts her husband's professional skill. There are no "stars," and everyone monitors his own work. At the same time, Julia says she needs to be ultimately in control: "I don't work well, if I'm not working for myself." Several years ago, when we first spoke, Julia was not as confident as a mother as she was of her role as wife and executive. But she was and is very proud of her daughter's independence and ability to make important decisions at a young age, as when she chose to go to boarding school. Still, Julia feels badly that one of the reasons her daughter may have wanted to go away was that Julia's mothering skills were not adequate. Not long ago, when we talked again, seven years and much therapy had passed. Julia's daughter had followed her in architectural interests. Today, they have much in common.

Moreover, one of Julia's major feelings of satisfaction is her marriage. She is happy to have found a man who both supports the career in which she excels and helps make her professional and private life more fulfilling.

Julia talked a bit about what women want. Early in women's lives they focus on romance and fulfillment through men. But, recently, she has heard many of her women friends talk about their need for intimacy with other women friends. The reality is that women live longer and outlive the images of romance and crave a different kind of intimacy. "I see much anger between the sexes. Women are looking to other women."

When asked if that was true of her, she declined to comment, saying she felt unusual and lucky in her choice of a mate.

Professionally, she says it gets better for her, "As you get older, you get freer."

Institutional Support

Rosabeth Kanter's book *Men and Women of the Corporation* offers the thesis that social behavior is shaped by the relative opportunities present within an existing social structure. Achievement is linked to opportunity, power and majority rule. Thus women and minorities have been at a disadvantage when one considers their position in the professional ranks. Because their numbers are still relatively small, they stand out, which inhibits them from taking calculated risks. It simply stands to reason that the organizations that provide opportunity for women to comfortably work together with men, go a long way toward making superior achievement possible. Interestingly, the women interviewed report support from their institutions by a ratio of three to one.

Family Attitudes: Confidence

Many women testified to the comfort they derived in adult life from supportive childhoods. They recall being gently indoctrinated with the same message: "You can be anything you want." A pilot remembers that the overriding message she received from both her parents was that she should try to be the best she could be, no matter what she did. A business executive said it was great, as a kid, "having every single person in your environment telling you 'you're the greatest.' "

Since many of the women had never encountered sexual discrimination until they began working, in some ways their supportive upbringing gave them a mantle of naivete. However, these early strokes ultimately served them well. They learned to say to people who judged them prematurely, "That's your problem."

As a jet pilot, Lynn Ripplemeyer experienced this kind of resistance from her colleagues, especially older veterans. She found it was comforting to have two female roommates at home base, with whom she could share her stories and compare notes. She also enjoyed the camaraderie of the International Women Pilots' Association.

"I never once considered that it wasn't worth it," she says. "Even in the bad times, I was learning about other people and how to communicate." She remembers she had especially good rapport with the flight attendants, who were surprisingly supportive. She had expected resentment from them, but instead their attitude was, "If you can do it, we can too."

It has only been within the last year or two that she has felt the reaction to a woman in the cockpit becoming more positive. She now gets reinforcement from both men and women. Why does she think this is so? "Because," she says, "it's no longer cool to be a male chauvinist.

"It has changed in the last five years. The most exciting thing is getting to see society grow up. Men get more comfortable as women get more comfortable with their freedom, choices, and roles. Men change in response to women and are freed of some of the responsibility they have had. They are freed of the role of care taker."

She found support in the helpful feedback of the male pilot who instructed her in the art of being a captain. He said she had to find subtle ways of making it clear who was in charge. He used the analogy of ballroom dancing: you know the music and rhythm, but, if you're leading, you have to make it fun. Since women are not taught to lead in the same way males are, one has to think it's okay. That way, everyone else will happily follow. "You need helpful feedback from people who understand the situation and you have to take it as helpful, not as criticism."

A Tale of Two Pilots

When Lynn was training to be a commercial pilot, there was one other woman in her Boeing 737 training class. They became friends, and, when they both returned to qualify on a 747, again found themselves classmates. Quickly, they realized only one of them could be "first" to fly one of the giant planes, and our respondent told her friend that she would be willing to delay her training if being first was important to the other.

The woman said no; she'd rather they qualify together. The two solidified their friendship and left it to the fates as to who would be scheduled to take the controls first. Recalling the situation, she said, "It was not worth it for me to be the first female to pilot a 747 and have problems with my friend." Instead, they rooted for each other.

Problems With Supporters

One television executive interviewed is in an enviable position. She has a high-powered job, and a husband who is extremely ambitious for her. However, she thinks there is a paradox created by his support. She feels propelled, through his drive, to work compulsively, to earn more, and to continue on a fast track. It has motivated her beyond her natural inclinations. On the other hand, she is concerned that his support not create a false standard for her so that she winds up living his dreams instead of her own. In other words, she may be supported on a course she might not have chosen on her own. As in many other situations, support may not come without some strings attached.

Working environments can also be insensitive to varying styles of doing business. A case in point was provided by a top female financial manager, who was very capable, but who scored low in self-confidence. At the request of her firm, she was attempting to become more "aggressive." She had been labeled "too nice." Unfortunately, while concentrating so diligently on being more direct and firm, she virtually erased one of her valuable assets, her friendliness. The criticism of her "niceness" undermined whatever other support she was getting.

Thus, organizational support is usually invaluable, but it can also carry a price. The important point for these women, however, is they were glad to have had the backing of supporters who aided them in various ways in their expanding roles.

Finding a Balance

A tale reported by Governor Madeleine Kunin of Vermont tells of both her spousal and early parental support.

"There is no single formula. It is a personal decision how one combines husband, children and career. You have to listen to your own inner voice about the proper sense of timing. I had my kids in a different era. I have four children. I had a ten-year period of my life which I spent juggling many obligations, both as a parent and as a student, going back to school. When my youngest child was two years old, I first ran for the legislature. And even that job was not a year round responsibility. I had good child care help. The most important thing is to feel comfortable that your children are getting good care. I did go through many periods of being torn between home and public life. Politics involves many nights and weekends.

"But there are no scars, and now my children encourage me to be involved, because they are older. Kids are happier if their parents are happy. My husband, as time went on, was increasingly involved in the rearing of the kids. He has grown along with me. But it's not like in the story books. There are difficulties.

"Women need more flexibility. The more flexibility there is, the better it is for women to combine both family and career. They need to be able to take work home, to have child care in the work place and maternity leaves. The business community is moving too slowly. If it was more accommodating, there would be higher productivity, more loyalty. It should be okay to have different tracks during different times of one's life.

"I didn't build a career. My decision to run for the legislature was spurred by a combination of the women's movement and the environment movement. As the kids got older, I got more involved. I came of age as doors opened for women. I couldn't have done this ten years ago.

"Between the ages of twenty-five and thirty, I had four kids, and I was not a professional person. Some say I lost time, but I decided, 'I am going back to school.' And got a master's degree. Also, being a parent adds dimensions to my work life which I have used: patience, humility, mediation skills and learning to not take yourself or your power too seriously.

"Women need different goals. But they have to have bosses that are flexible. As women work their way up the ladder, hopefully those women who enter positions of power will be understanding and help other women coming along to define more effective ways women can work.

"There is something humanizing about being a parent that is beneficial to the work place. My being a woman and parent is not a separate part of my life. It is blended and part of my focus as governor, reflected in my priorities: education, child care and prenatal care. Those issues have a certain intensity because of my life experiences as a woman."

When asked if she worked differently because she is a woman, Kunin replied, "Yes. But it is difficult to separate gender out. Undoubtedly there are some differences, such as how one reacts emotionally to conflict, how one gathers information and seeks advice. Most women haven't been trained to steel themselves emotionally. It's still a learning process. I'm constantly learning how to deal more effectively with conflict. However, I don't believe this is always easy for men either. They may simply be less likely to reveal their discomfort with their leadership decisions."

I asked her how she prevailed, "Partly, I have an inner drive that makes me want to lead a full life. I never wanted not to be a parent, but *only* being a parent does not work for me. I am intellectually curious and want to help shape events. And the more I do—the more steps I take— the more positive reinforcement I get to do more. I think many people have the same desires, and I don't know what happens to make them forsake or modify those goals.

"In my case, my immigrant experience gave me a sense of opportunity. And growing up without a father lent a certain necessity to independence and becoming myself."

Extended Parenting

Increased participation in parenting by one's partner is certainly, in many cases we studied, a major component making it possible to function well as parent and wife, and excel in business pursuits. In many situations we studied, where a single parent is involved, other support mechanisms, such as grandparents, siblings, aunts, uncles and friends assume important roles in children's lives and extend the family support systems.

Moreover, traditional definitions of maternal/paternal functions become blurred—the available parent assuming the nurturing role when needed.

CHAPTER SIX

STRATEGIES FOR THE FAST TRACK

"As you get older, you have to be a little more direct, a little less wieldy. We're all raised to be nice, but sometimes you don't have the time. I have no choice. I have to get from A to B. But you get funnier; your sense of humor blossoms."

Marcy Carsey
—Producer of "Cosby," "Roseanne"

To satisfy both their ambitions and family responsibilities, many of the women in this study have changed careers, jobs or specialties. Some no longer work in the field for which they were originally trained or educated. A high percentage have changed their geographic location. The mobility they exhibit comes from new attempts to work out individual success formulas which synchronize with their family goals. The pattern of flexibility woven by these women reflects their attempts to find the most challenging roles permitted by their talents and society while they still fulfill family responsibilities. The formula which most have found satisfying gratifies both needs.

In order to achieve success having the added component of family life, some women have had to give up their original goals and substitute new ones with different but equal challenges. The reasons they give for job changes include efforts to find work they enjoy, accommodating family needs, working with compatible institutions and colleagues, reducing stress, augmenting power, taking advantage of changing social context, attempting a multitude of more individualized endeavors, and finding unique opportunities for attaining high level positions while still fulfilling family needs. Being bright and ambitious these women wrestled with the question of how to achieve their goals after having children; some returned to professional schools or began new businesses in their own homes. Others struggled to reduce stress by relinquishing part of their professional demands—resigning law partnerships or giving up careers in medicine are only two examples.

In all these coping mechanisms, some tension remains between the dual demands of work and home life. There is tension between the push for accomplishment, stimulation and contribution and the desire for serenity, satisfaction, family time and relaxation. As these women navigate between these two extremes, they often retrench and regroup in both areas before moving forward again.

Among their stories many common attitudes surfaced—a responsibility to society, potentials, using inborn gifts, the need for family life, leisure time and meditation. Despite these sometimes conflicting attitudes, there are common behaviors that pushed and propelled these women up the ladder of success.

Deliberate Steady Push for Challenge

Hard work is a theme repeated endlessly and matter-of-factly, verbally or in describing their daily drive and commitment. A newscaster sums it up: "I give 110 percent. I just figure if you want to be a cowboy, you have to ride the range." Her story includes the endless extra hours volunteered in preparing herself for her big break. She spent hours, without being asked, in the library and in the newsroom, studying television reporting. When a story broke, she was ready, and no other more experienced anchors were present.

Surgeon Marjorie Fine had been a housewife for

years prior to her decision to enter medical school. She found that spending all her time with two small children was boring. She was "ironing the walls". She found she was so enthusiastic and stimulated by school that it was easier to get through the routine parts of her day. In terms of work, she feels she had always done other things and assumed it was for money or role fulfillment. "But (medical school) was something I wanted to do. The years away from school matured me so I was focused."

However, Fine says realistically, "when you start you don't know what you are getting into." She describes her residency with two young children at home as brutal. According to Fine, nothing was more difficult. "The first year of my internship was the most horrible." She spent every other night in the hospital until 10 a.m. and then left home at 6 p.m. to return to work. On alternate nights as well as alternate weekends, she stayed in the hospital. But she says, "when you are so embroiled in the process, it is just as easy to get through it as to get out of it."

Bank executive Dianne Arnold felt she wanted to work and did so right after college. After her first child was born, she took six months off and came back to work two days a week and gradually worked her way up to full time by the end of two years. (There had been no prior experience at her bank with maternity leave.) At the end of this two year period, she decided she wanted to do something to put herself on the fast track and made a deliberate decision to push for a position in commercial banking. This position involved a lot of travel, but, after two years of more focused child care, she was eager and ready.

Being Prepared

Martina Whitman attributes some of her success to *taking advantage of the opportunities when they come along.* She accepted an important job in Washington, D.C., even though the timing was not the best for her young family. Whitman went from college professor to being a member of the President's Economic Council and then a top executive at General Motors.

The aspect of preparedness—not only by academic and work experience but by providing for family care—is paramount according to the women surveyed. A gradual networking of family tasks and a shared atmosphere of responsibility is necessary to enable a woman to reach her career goals.

Finding a Compatible Institution

Most women were very deliberate about seeking and finding compatible work environments. Many gave great forethought to the kinds of organization that would fit into their families' and professional needs. Some had to make one or more career changes to find compatible institutions.

Carol Dinkins' husband was a partner in a big law firm and she saw first hand the rigorous requirement of hours and dedication. Having two small children, she knew she couldn't commit that kind of time. She was also aware that there were not many married women with children in big corporate law firms. She wanted to pick a legal field where there were more opportunities for achievement, flexibility and individuality. She found a college faculty position with regular limited hours and no travel. That excellent choice resulted, along with hard work and competence, in developing a specialty in a new field, environmental law, which has come center stage in our national life and priorities in the 1990s. She is now at the core of that area and is in great demand. Her children are also well launched, so she can devote more time to the professional life she has developed.

Marcy Carsey went to ABC television when it was rated third out of three major networks. She was also pregnant. At that time, ABC had to fight hard for recognition and ratings. They badly needed new talent. Marcy knew she had made a good decision when she mentioned in her initial interview with Michael Eisner that she was pregnant and he said, "Oh, good, I'm going to have a child too."

Sharon Flaherty "fits" into her organization, Kaiser Permanente. Her values—she is a very value-oriented person—and her goals are compatible with those of the organization, which is concerned with doing the right thing and also value driven.

Jennifer Lawson says she has been lucky to work for five years for organizations which have been respectful of women and people of color. In her organization, women hold top positions and influence the corporate culture. However, Jennifer has also been active in insuring the growth of that receptiveness when she became Affirmative Action Coordinator and ombudsman. At that time she was able to ferret out any discriminatory concerns before they became permanent.

Marcy Tiffany, FTC Regional Director, thrashed about a good bit and changed jobs about every two years. She has finally landed a top government position. "I feel blessed. I could make twice as much money in private law firms but, in my job, I am home by six. Here your job is to get your job done. In private business you have to go out and drum up business in your spare time, and they worry about billable hours. I am lucky because, even though I make less money, I have fascinating legal work and still have a prestige position while having time for my family concerns." Being in a smaller office, Marcy finds it is possible to be more informal and operate more humanely as far as flexible time for her staff and herself. But she did not come to this position accidentally. She expended great effort to make the right career move to satisfy both personal and work needs.

Elizabeth Blalock went to Kaiser Permanente because she did not want the full responsibility of a private practice. She did not want to run her own business because, as a single parent, she was aware of her children's competing needs.

Barbara Corday left her successful writing partnership to take a lower-salaried job as a network executive—against the advice of her husband and agent—so that she could get necessary management experience and distinguish herself as an individual.

Plenty of dust flew as these women changed positions in order to find work they loved as well as to fulfil family responsibilities. Many of the moves were enacted because they were eager to utilize their limited available time to *connect* with work they embraced. Fulfilling their dual needs, these women were able to *attribute positive meaning* to their work identities but also were able to be flexible, moving until they landed compatible situations. During their journeys many often paused to reassess their goals and then moved again when it seemed necessary.

One producer started out as a teacher, a profession for which she had been trained, but found her heart was in commercial and creative areas. She seized an opportunity to use her skills in education as a program evaluator for the new video disk commercial industry and entered the world of creative production. By doing a good job in a small division, she was promoted to president and reorganized company procedures so that reaching business goals rather than fulfilling rigid time requirements became a priority.

Tales of Courage
These women forged new paths and most tell brave tales. One producer was able to transcend her teacher's salary and her own expectations when negotiating the contract for her new position as president. Her predecessor earned approximately $250,000 per year. As Educational Assistant, she was earning about $30,000. After a short time, she was asked for her salary requirements and remembers practicing saying $75,000 a year out loud in front of a mirror three or four times a day just so that she could utter the figure in real negotiation.

Merrie Spaeth relates her story of valor that also turned out to be a great strategy. She was appointed, clearly as a token female member, to a very prestigious economic development commission staffed with old, blue-blood males. At the first meeting, the Chairman introduced the new board members including a Japanese man whose name he badly mispronounced. As a communications specialist, Merrie couldn't help herself. She approached the Chairman and said, "Do us all a favor. The next time you don't know how to pronounce a name, you either find out how to pronounce it in advance or ask us to do it ourselves." Regretting her candor later, Merrie thought that her lack of tact had sealed her fate in the worst way. Several months later she found herself appointed to an even more prestigious board at the Dallas/Ft. Worth airport and discovered that the same Chairman to whom she had made her forthright remarks had recommended her. When, some time later, she finally got the opportunity to ask why, he explained that he knew she would stand up for the Board when they needed someone who wasn't afraid to protect their interests. "I wish I had realized that twenty five years ago," she now remarks.

Great Individual Effort in Job Search Position

Many of the women with whom we spoke described expending great individual effort in their chosen careers.

Doctor Helen Blumin said, "When I first started, I worked hard, pounded on doors, gave my cards. I had to be politically active at the hospital. I deliberately read the sports page. Once you have the patients to refer, then you have power."

Marcy Tiffany pushed her own career. "I pulled out every stop, called on everybody I knew, and earned that job by finding it and engineering it. Maybe it was my willingness to take a step out. I made concerted efforts, talked to people, found the job and lobbied. I am tempted to say I was damned lucky, but that wasn't the case. If the break didn't go my way, I focused my energy, said 'I want this,' and went after it."

Marcy did this once after she worked a short time in

a law firm but did not like the litigation. "I couldn't get enthusiastic fighting over other people's money," she said, "so I put feelers out." Marcy eventually took what might have looked like a step backward, but what was in reality an interesting clerkship with an excellent woman judge.

She was proactive then in moving to Washington, thinking it would be a good interim step to further her career with another law firm. Again, she found she did not like the law firm environment and actively sought the position of Antitrust Council and Chief Economist on the Senate Judiciary Committee. Attaining that goal, she went on to another job in government as executive assistant to the FTC chairman.

Changing Jobs

A strong recurring theme in this study is the number of women who changed jobs and even careers: sixty-seven percent had significant job changes and fifty percent changed careers. Women went from stockbroker to politician, from college professor to newspaper executive, from teacher to lawyer or television producer, from private practice doctor to sales person, from obstetrical to gynecological surgery specialists. The study found that they were not frightened to make changes that would be more satisfactory, productive or place them in responsive environments.

Marcy Tiffany and her husband decided to move back to California so that he could accept a position as a Federal judge and to be near family who could help in raising their children. At this point she chose to be general counsel to Guess Jeans. "I pulled out all the stops to find that job," she said. But, unfortunately, it was not satisfying. Undaunted, she launched a drive to find a new position.

One successful businesswoman finally left a company where she felt she had been unfairly treated and unfairly compensated. Another, Doctor Blalock, left her job and her chief assignment so that she could live in Laguna Beach, which she felt would be more satisfying for her family. A third, Helen Blumin sold her medical practice after ten successful years because she did not want the continuing demands of a partnership in a private business.

Finding Supportive People

Finding people who could help these successful women reach their goals was an important component of their later success. Astronaut Fisher's ability to prevail in her "part time" request was partially the result of informal lobbying on her behalf by several supportive male colleagues. Barbara Boxer went to supportive male colleagues to follow up and persevere in her request for the integration of the Congressional gym—after she had been turned down by the old male guard.

Partners

Many of the women in independent business chose to work with compatible partners so they could share difficult work assignments and time commitments.

Marcy Carsey's strategy involved sharing responsibilities and burdens. She was like a doctor on call, but only for half the time. She and her partner alternated trips to New York, lessening the burdens, releasing energy and making it possible for each to fulfill family responsibilities.

Changing Directions

The realities of family life make it important for ambitious women to be able to change directions if one job or institution will not permit them to fulfil all their responsibilities. It is also important to be able to make such changes with a positive attitude.

Geraldine Ferraro, who was in business for herself at the time, was able to take time off to be with her dying mother. "If they still want me to give a speech six weeks from now, fine. If they don't, I'll do something else."

Following Your Interest

Barbara Boxer went to work for a nearby newspaper so her hours, schedule and commute would be compatible with that of her family. When Boxer is asked by young women how they can become a Congresswoman, she tells them not to start out with that in mind. "I got involved by following the issues and my interests."

Marjorie Fine loves being a surgeon and believes she can make people's lives better. Astronaut Anna Fisher thrills audiences when talking about her love for the space program, her hopes for the future of mankind and her dreams of international cooperation.

Create Your Own Life

These women created innovative, workable life/family work patterns. Some had stay-at-home husbands who were the primary nurturers. Others lived, for periods of time, in cities separate from their spouse or children. Barbara Corday has not been in a grocery store in six years. Ellen Gordon's daughter was enrolled in two schools in two cities simultaneously.

Nancy Evans tells her story: "When I got pregnant, I immediately installed a fax and a secretary at home and developed a schedule for messengers, so I could operate from home. Everybody came to my house. They loved it. And we got so much more accomplished. When you are in the office, there are all kinds of interruptions—the phones are ringing. But when they had to trek downtown to my house, they were more comfortable. You could drink a soda. There was no resistance to this for me—but there was resistance for the women in positions below mine."

One of the most important components of making their lives work is the ability not to think in stereotypes but to invent their own lifestyle patterns.

Deliberate Choices for Hard Temporary Duty

Carol Dinkins talks about her four years commuting between her job in Washington D.C. and her young family in Houston. "It's not my favorite lifestyle, it's just one of those things. It was hard, but it was a wonderful once-in-a-lifetime opportunity that I felt I did not want to miss."

Marjorie Fine got through medical school while rearing small children. Astronaut Anna Fisher took a flight in space with a fifteen-month-old youngster at home. Barbara Boxer served her first year in Congress with active teenagers at home.

The ability to accept less than adequate temporary solutions and to work for more satisfying long terms ones is a quality most successful women in this survey share.

Resisting Jobs Incompatible with Interests

One executive talked of refusing a seemingly big promotion in her video disc division where she would have overseen a large budget and staff in the production of training discs. She favored keeping her small staff and budget for speculative commercial creative productions. It was a strategic career gamble that paid off in eventual success in the area of her dreams, commercial production.

A television producer resigned from her successful post as president of a Movie of the Week with a large network where she had a guaranteed salary and prestige position to pursue her love of independent production. Within a year she had a critically acclaimed feature film to her credit.

Dentist Nancy Schort regulates her practice so she can take more time with each patient, denying the temptation of greater volume and money in deference to her concept of quality care.

The Unusual Career Ladder—Down

One especially ambitious lawyer is perhaps the most unusual example of driving hard and straight to the top only to find that the top is not where she really wanted to be. She graduated first in her law school class, worked right through her first marriage and lived for a year in a different city from her family while she finished her degree. She was a classic workaholic. She pushed during these long hours to become one of the first female partners in a prestigious Los Angeles law firm. After her first child was born, she created an odd niche for herself by choosing to work as a partner—but only two-thirds of the time. Then she resigned and became a law clerk working on special projects for her former colleagues. Finally, she realized her job had become unfulfilling and resigned totally.

"I am contented now," she says. "I don't miss the job. I felt law was boring and anxiety producing. It made me crazy to have to be mean all the time. I didn't get anything out of being a mucky-muck and I have never regretted the decision of resigning."

Helen Blumin provides another example of changing goals by selling her successful ongoing medical practice after ten years. Subsequently she entered the medical marketing field where she is much more satisfied.

Deliberate Strategies for Reducing Stress

Because of her family commitments, after fourteen years Amy Roseman forsook her original goal of an obstetrical practice, focused on gynecology and developed a whole new interest in the specialty of female incontinence.

Yvonne Burke, a former member of Congress, discusses scaling back. "I had to make a decision early on to have a 'hands on' relationship with my daughter. I was in Congress when she was born, and they liked to say she had 434 godmothers and godfathers. Everyone was very excited and supportive. People were excited; she was the adopted kid of Congress."

Yvonne was forty when her daughter was born. She had remarried at thirty-eight and had discussed wanting a child and being committed to a new family life with her

STRATEGIES FOR THE FAST TRACK

husband. He had a daughter, now twenty-two, by a former marriage, who lived part of the time with them.

"I took my daughter everywhere I went. I had baby-sitters all over the country—and world; I took her to China when she was nine months old. I had two of everything—in Los Angeles and Washington, D.C. I had a live-in in Washington where she went to pre-school, and someone always on call in Los Angeles. I took her on the campaign trail with me when she was three. Maybe that's why she's not interested in politics."

Her daughter is now sixteen. Yvonne's unusual decision not to run again for Congress had "in large part" to do with the fact that her ability to be with her daughter was made very difficult because of having to live in two places. Usually, Yvonne left the Capitol every Thursday evening and returned Sunday night. Because California and Washington, D.C. are so far apart, she had more travel time, less rest and less family life than some of her colleagues.

A lot of small and large compromises detail the ways in which successful women have tried to balance family needs and work life and still satisfy their ultimate desires of making effective contributions and fulfilling their career goals.

Clearing Your Own Path

According to the women surveyed, sometimes the best strategy is to define one's own path several times along the journey. Anna Fisher is in the process of doing just that right now, as she carves out a part-time position in NASA. Dianne Arnold went back to work on a part-time basis in 1971 after her first child was born, at a time when the company's basic policy was that women did not return to work after having children. Although her rigid work style changed, she continued to fulfill her work goals by creating a new, more flexible style.

Original goals are not always satisfying or realistic as one's lifestyle develops—especially when the realities of marriage, children and employment make their own demands. New objectives need to be set and flexibility maintained if all the component parts of an evolving family life and work life are to be satisfied.

Deliberate Education

Despite, or perhaps because of, their complex needs and responsibilities, the women in this survey made sure to get information and make strategic contacts that would augment their careers with the addition of family concerns. A newspaper executive returned to school for an MBA when her Ph.D. did not ensure the kind of employment which accommodated her other needs. She also deliberately joined groups where she could make important contacts with firms which would complement her ambitions.

Sandra Day O'Connor found great help in joining professional women's groups where they discussed similar work, family issues and problems. She both learned from these experiences and received comfort from the participants.

Jennifer Lawson was admitted to graduate school without finishing undergraduate studies. When she started in management she felt naive about management issues and strategically educated herself by reading the available books and articles in that area.

Lita Albuquerque deliberately changed some lifestyle attitudes—like feeling guilty about being away from her children and having live-in help—after attending "Mommy and Me" sessions.

Amy Roseman designed sabbatical leave, patterning her business for all the partners to take advantage of the same "perks" she needed to fulfill her family obligation.

Learning Politics

Two excellent examples are given in the following stories that strategically point out effective strategies. Barbara Boxer wanted to have use of the all-male Congressional gym. Two years passed. She was told she couldn't.

Then she prevailed with some of her younger male friends who approached the gym committee. This endorsement and her follow-up allowed her to be taken more seriously. (Also, one of the older committee members had an athletic wife.) Boxer mentioned, as did other women, that humor is often an effective strategy. Sung to the tune of "Five Foot Two," she used humor in a plea to get her point across about the Congressional gym:

> Exercise, glamorize
> Where to go
> Will you advise
> Can't everybody use your gym?
> We're not trim, we're not slim,
> Can't you make it hers and him
> Can't everybody use your gym?

A dentist wanted to be on the Board of Dental Examiners. She states you have to study the unwritten rules in order to gain entry into difficult positions of male supremacy. She got her appointment by the Governor of the State of California by calling everyone in the state who might know someone who knew the Governor. By networking her contacts and his friends she was able to sell herself.

In reaching her job goals within Michael Dukakis' campaign, Susan Estrich did not complain about being left out or having hurt feelings. "It's not their job to monitor my feelings." If she was excluded from an important political lunch, she did not complain. She reached out to those who were included, saying simply, "I understand you had a lunch in which you discussed some important matters and this is how I feel about the issue."

The moral of these stories involves being seen as well as effectively pleading your case to others of significant importance. As Barbara Boxer said, "use persistence, patience and humor, but be ready to demand."

Using Your Background and Experiences

Several women extensively used both their childhood and early experiences as they ascended the career ladder. Sandra Day O'Connor grew up on a ranch and learned independence by taking care of her own needs. According to her, those lessons served her well when she became the first woman justice of the Supreme Court.

Geraldine Ferraro and Jennifer Lawson learned through adversity because of the early deaths of one of their parents. Lawson talks about learning survival so that later defeats were seen as momentary and not final. Ferraro strove to get out of the South Bronx and get an education. Once attaining that goal, her response to adversity was to work fourteen and fifteen hour days and push herself until her initial goals were attained.

Governor Kunin of Vermont says that "My being a woman and parent is not a separate part of my life. It is blended and part of my focus of Governor reflected in my priorities: education, child care and prenatal care. Those issues have my intensity. Some say I lost time from age twenty-five to thirty-five while I was raising my four kids, but being a parent adds a dimension that includes patience, humility, mediation skills and learning not to take yourself or your power too seriously."

The President of Tootsie Roll, Ellen Gordon who has four children, took considerable time off and dropped out of school after the birth of her first child. She went back to school between her third and fourth child and then on to graduate school. But basically she was a wife and mother for many years. "I don't consider that a stagnant period. I learned so much about people and interactions. It is an important learning process and a very creative time."

Making Demands and Proving Themselves

According to the women in this survey, the ability to verbalize effectively changes that ought to be made to make the work environment more supportive of women in general—and to family oriented women in particular—is an essential ingredient of success.

Most women told stories of hard work in which they proved their commitment and dedication prior to taking maternity time off or scaling back after having children.

One of the women interviewed was director of a major Wall Street firm and earned her MBA from an ivy league college in a year and a half. She was married when she was twenty-five years old, as she got out of business school. She wanted to continue working. "I wanted a long term career and wanted to keep active in my job. I wanted financial independence."

Her father was a supermarket executive who eventually became president of the firm. He always encouraged her working. Her mother had been a nurse. She had begun her career at another firm, but felt she shouldn't have children right away because she wanted to establish her career. Her husband is seven years older. His company wanted him to go to France; her company offered her a job in France. She thought, "I really do want a family and am ready. Working in Europe might be less pressured."

They had their first child in 1977. She took off three months for which she was paid, although the firm did not have a maternity policy at the time. The couple had a wonderful nurse.

But people kept saying to her, "If you want a long term career, you really ought to come back to New York." Finally, she said to her husband, "Look, you had a shot at it, and I want to have the same opportunity." He was very supportive and told her if that's what she wanted, she should go for it. His firm offered him a job in New York.

She moved to sales, which she found more tempered. "I'm better at selling and managing my own time figuring out what a business is worth. It gave me some flexibility. But, I did that under conditions which were unpleasant. When I didn't get a bonus, they said, 'Well, you're a woman and your husband works.' But it was still good money, I liked the work and I was somewhat independent.

"We never had live-in help. My husband and I were interchangeable at tasks of administration and nurturing. He is fantastic with the kids."

She continued in sales and had another child in 1982. Again, she had a three months paid maternity leave, during which time she nursed the baby.

"By then I'd 'had it' not being appreciated."

Finally, she went in to her superiors and said, "Look, this is not right. I don't think I am being paid properly and my boss isn't supportive." This conversation took place in front of her (unsupportive) boss and his superior. Shortly thereafter, the superior to whom she complained asked her to run the retail division with the Managing Director title she had requested.

When the company merged, "It was so exciting to have a new group and more responsibility. I could throw myself into the new situation." At this time her children were seven and two.

But, in 1988, there was another change and she lost the position as head of retailing. She decided that, aside from not being paid properly, her supporters had left. She accepted another executive position in an area of the company where there was a tremendously cooperative atmosphere and more creative opportunities.

What made her successful? "Perseverance, sticking with it. Plus I liked the financial rewards." When asked if there were any differences in her style as opposed to that of a man's, she answered, "The most important is a sensitivity to people. For example, when dealing with sales of companies owned by people with big egos—in a situation that can be adversarial—I use persuasion rather than aggression. I have found my style and difference and use it. I know who I am. It took me a while to get the Managing Director job. I saw a lot of women who did change their style along the way. But I was never willing to compromise."

She earns more money than her husband, but they are co-equal in valuing what they do. She works from about 8:00 a.m. until 7:30 p.m. and often travels. "But the girls seem to understand it. I always call and they understand traveling is part of my job. Maybe one tip is that I never complain. It's taken as a matter of course. Weekends are spent with them all the time, day and evening. They don't feel they are being ignored."

She offers these tips: "It's important to establish yourself early on in your career. I delayed having kids and it stood me well in the 'lean' years. I was viewed as hard working, cooperative. People felt they could count on me. If you want to combine career and family, maybe you should postpone parenting a little bit—but not too much.

"Space your kids. I saw the amount of effort I put into the first child and realized the amount of time I wanted to put in with my second and needed to be able to take time from my worklife to do that.

"Find a husband who doesn't get his ego out of joint. My husband just pitches in, almost as a natural thing. Sometimes he cleans the table after dinner and sometimes I do. We just flow.

"Fortunately, we don't have a lot of money problems. He doesn't travel, and we don't do a lot of socializing. Sometimes we talk about business, but not a lot.

"Once you are close to the top, it's easier. It's the beginning years that are really difficult. You have to remember every career has ups and downs, and some women just quit when they are down.

"Women of the nineties will have an easier time, as their male peers will also have wives who work outside the home."

Successful family-oriented women executives and entrepreneurs have to manage their home lives in such a way as to maintain clear consciences. Yvonne Burke finally quit Congress because she could not work comfortably with her dual responsibilities and took a chance on running for the post of Attorney General to keep her commuting distance to a one hour plane flight within her home state.

Debbie Fields' husband travels with her ninety-nine percent of the time and her children accompany her on a great many trips. She arranges activities for the children while she visits one of her stores; she knows they are having a good experience while she is working; thus her mind is clear. She doesn't have business dinners out, but rather "invites people in even if they have to partake of spaghetti and spilled milk."

Flexibility

"I fell into things." This is a statement by a woman who achieved one of the highest positions in our national public life. She is Madeleine Kunin, Governor of Vermont. She had no grand strategy. "I don't really know how I did it," she said. "As a kid I had no idea I would pursue a career in politics later in life. When I came of age, doors were beginning to open for women. I couldn't have done what I have done if I came along ten years earlier or maybe even ten years later."

It is helpful and encouraging to see that by a combination of drive, dedication and curiosity, a mother of four can fulfill her work ambitions without great preplanning. "Partly, I have this inner drive that makes me want to lead a full life," Kunin explains. "I never wanted to *not* be a parent but *only* being a parent did not work for me. I had an intellectual curiosity and desire to shape events. I think many people have the same desire and I really don't know what happens to them to make them put that desire on the back burner." Whatever the original impetus, her strategy was to fulfill her inner needs and progress.

The ability to be flexible, to adapt, to change and to use the experience life brings to formulate new opportunities and goals is what these women's success stories have in common. They all maintain that without one simple component—flexibility—their current prosperity in business and happy family lives could not have occurred.

Foundations

These women *have* and *have created* support. Many of the women in this study married early, but some of them divorced husbands who did not support their careers. They would not allow themselves to remain in marriages that held them back.

The kind of support and attribution to the assistance of support was widespread. Thirty-five percent had mates in the same field and could discuss business with them. Fifteen percent said their husbands were the primary nurturer of the children. Successful women in this survey describe amazing care and support in family obligations and child care duties.

Great diversity is the theme in the kinds of support and the way these women held their marriages together during periods of near total dedication to their careers.

Marcy Carsey, executive producer of Carsey Werner Productions and producer of "The Bill Cosby Show" and "Roxanne," offers these insights into her fast track performance while juggling motherhood.

When asked about the potential negative impact of her work demands on her softer personna, she responded, "As you get older, you have to be a little more direct, a little less wieldy. We're all raised to be nice, but you don't have the time. You have to be more direct and you get over some of that instinctive fear of taking a position. I have no choice. I have to get from A to B. But you get funnier; your sense of humor blossoms."

It was hard for her to be specific when asked if women are different as managers. "A little less corporate, a lot less by the book." Her examples: "You push responsibility down in the organization; delegate. When people come with a problem, I always say, 'Well, let's see, what would you like to do about that,' and they *always* have the answers within them. I tend to involve everyone I can—to learn from and contribute."

She could pinpoint the differences between her style

and that of her male partner specifically, but not necessarily as generally illustrative of the differences between males and females. Her partner will approach a problem directly: "that is the focus; let's get to solving it." Her own approach: "Let's put it aside a bit and look at other things in the interim."

Marcy's attitudes about help are also different. For example, "Many people refer to this as a Mom and Pop company and I guess that suggests differing roles. I am tougher when it gets to the bottom line. I will stand on principle—sometimes even to the point of obnoxiousness. I defend my own people."

But her partner enables her to live a saner life. They divide their responsibilities literally like a medical tag team.

Marcy was married at twenty-four to a man twenty-three years her senior: "A guy who will let me do all that stuff—do whatever. We are soul mates and friends. I knew more definitely then that I wanted to have children and that I wanted to work." When it was suggested that her choice of a mate was luck, she quickly responded that she avoided the kind of guys who were saying, "Let's get married and you put me through medical school, and so forth." She is now forty-five and has a daughter fifteen and a son twelve. "The girl is so unlike me. She is like a beloved stranger. You think you know what's best for them and you don't know. I remember a few years ago when she came home with a few B's and C's. I spoke to her. You shouldn't be getting these kind of grades; you're a bright girl and can do better. And you don't want to do anything to limit your options. I will never forget the look on her face. I didn't understand until a long time later that this bright, intense, worried little girl was trying to find balance in her young life and had just swung a little too far in the other direction trying to make friends, reach out."

When Marcy's firm began producing "The Bill Cosby Show," it was in New York. "The first year was the hardest. It was hard to be away. I was gone half the time for six years. Every week, I left Sunday night on the red eye and returned Friday on an early plane. I was always home on the weekends." This began when her kids were nine and six, and lasted from August through April. "It was very hard, but the work was such fun. And it was a conscious decision. The invitation was always there to the family to come with me, but they rarely took me up on it.

"I have no idea how this impacted the kids; I could only guess. I had been so vigilant about making up for lost time. But, at the end of the first season, my daughter said, 'Now that that is over, do you think we could spend a little less time together?' My guess is it was good for them because I tend to be a hoverer—a little like my mother, over controlling. They seemed to be okay, and it was only me that got on the plane each Sunday, feeling like I was going to cry.

"I got through it because I knew the time I did spend with them was more important than that of most housewives. For most women who don't work, time has a tendency to stretch out forever.

"No, I never had the impulse to quit. It would have been more tempting when I was young. Now it's easier. When you're more successful at the top, you can say, 'Hey, it's 2:40 p.m. I'm out of here. I'm going to pick up my son— probably continue the argument I had going with him this morning, take him to the bookstore' and we're off.

"Plus, I'm a great negotiator and a good delegator. For example, I hired two English sisters as caretakers for the kids. We didn't have room for them, but it didn't matter. We gave them the good room and put the kids together. I wanted a family atmosphere, and each sister worked a seven day shift and then traded off. It was a seven day schedule—like me and my partner. We never had to worry. It's covered.

"That's why I hire a lot of moms as line producers. They know the difference between a scratch and a life and death issue."

CHAPTER SEVEN

CORPORATE WORKSTYLES

"I have my secretary open the mail, and, if I have five minutes between meetings—five minutes dead time—I can handle some of the paperwork. You have to be very organized, make the most of every moment."

Debbie Smith
—Vice President
Xerox Corporation

A central issue of the 1990s is the workstyle needs of women as they cope with complex family roles and move into the higher ranks of organizational life and entrepreneurship. Just as women struggle to fulfill internal dictum to "be the best you can possibly be," to pursue adventure, contribution, and mastery, while searching for acceptance and domestic happiness, business institutions are struggling to gracefully integrate women into professions and organizations, while accommodating their family roles. We are all caught up in this social learning process for which there are no precedents, although some women have been more successful and some institutions more receptive. All the women described in this book have records of high achievement; however, some have achieved top positions within large scale organizations and corporation life, while others have risen in alternative workstyles. They have attained positions of responsibility and influence in which they have been able to assert their own styles rather than accommodate pre-established standards.

Pam Flaherty is an attractive woman with a relaxed manner and a smile that comes easily. She has a subtle sense of feminine style. She is also a top division executive of one of the largest and fastest growing bank systems in the nation—Citicorp. Approximately six thousand employees report to her.

Heading Citibank's Northeast Division, Flaherty has management responsibility for consumer, branch and business banking in the greater New York area, upstate New York and Maine.

"One of the luckiest things that happened to me at Citicorp was my first job here working for a Senior Vice President in a terrific staff job." Where else, she indicates, could a new employee get so much exposure to senior managers and, at the same time, a chance to exhibit her abilities to other high level managers.

"I learned early that the style at Citicorp is fast moving, dynamic, unorthodox." Flaherty feels a key to her success is a compatible fit between the organization she works for and herself.

Was being a woman a handicap to her ambitions? Flaherty's views are unorthodox on this subject.

"On the contrary, it helped. In the early years, if you had credentials for a job—and not too many women did then—it made you stand out. Anything that makes you stand out beyond the neutral, helps.

"Being a woman makes you colorful, and color's important for a woman. Most people describe me as a feminine woman. I always wear appropriate business clothes, but I like to add feminine touches. It's part of my over-all style. I tend to be polite and to listen and not raise my voice. I'm not harsh with people. A lot of women try to behave like men. I think I behave like myself. I'm more of a consensus manager than a confrontational one. If, let us say, there's an interoffice problem that requires a fairly drastic solution, I'm not one for forcing it on people, if I can help it. I prefer to implement solutions by either discussing it with them on a one-to-one basis or by getting them all into a room and working them into an agreement with whatever compromises are possible. With that technique, even if things don't end up their way, people feel more involved."

Aside from believing she has some femine traits, she thinks her way of handling situations could be part of the middle child syndrome. "I was a middle child and I think that's a part of what gives me an appetite for consensus. Not that I can't be forceful and crisp when needed.

"I don't shout. I've been told my way of being forceful is to radiate authority. I wonder if the feeling that the chair will always be under me when I sit down comes from the security of having made my career totally at Citicorp. I grew up in a big, rambling house in a suburb of St. Louis, and I went to the same high school attended by my mother and her mother."

Although Pam feels the career obstacles facing a woman in a corporation can be overcome, she does say that "as you get more senior, it becomes more of a problem. Dealing with top level people, the differences are more subtle. But, of course, the differences between men and women are not subtle." As for dealing with these problems, she shrugs, "No matter how you craft yourself, you are who and what you are, and you have to learn to leverage in your own style."

Pam's father was a doctor, her mother a nurse, but neither, according to her, is particularly her role model. Fundamentally, she feels that she was steered by her combined heritage towards always doing the best she can: respecting people and dealing openly with them. She makes a concentrated effort to learn from successful people.

Pam feels a great sense of partnership with her husband of twenty years in which they not only share common values and goals, but the responsibilities of their two children.

"When people ask me what my husband thinks

about me working, I'm always tempted to reply, 'What about what I think about my husband working?' "

Both feel that both family and profession are vitally important. "Life is very full, so full that I always feel pulled." Socializing is necessarily kept to a minimum except with the family. "The only cultural event seems to be Sesame Street."

Pam admits she is a workaholic, but sternly regulates her routine so as to be home as often as possible at 6:30. Her husband does the same.

"I don't feel guilty about my children. We feel comfortable that what our family is doing makes sense. I feel good about myself and have a supportive spouse and a good family life. The rest is logistics and making it work. We don't do a lot else. We give up social life for family life."

Her children are now eight and twelve. She took six weeks maternity leave with each one. She was anxious to get everybody back to normal and adjusted to a schedule because her working life was the norm. For a period of time, however, she reduced her hours and travel. Admitting there are many times in kids' lives when they need extra attention, she tries "to make whatever sacrifices are necessary to be there."

According to her, keys to her success include concentration on execution, getting a pending job completed, building a track record over time, talking to people, taking opportunities for participation, promoting one's self and creating the expectation of doing a good job.

Her advice to young women in the business world is, "I don't see any one answer or kind of behavior. There are multiple life styles. Results are usually much harder to come by than anticipated. The important thing is to learn and absorb and never stop. Reach out to other people in the organization. Never be shy about talking to people or taking problems to supervisors. They are the coaches. People above you have all done that in their time and probably still are. In between learning and absorbing, step back, now and then, and try to get perspective, because, in the end, your decisions must come out of you. Once you've learned, don't be afraid to trust yourself. When you have hard choices that appear beyond your acumen to solve, trust your instincts."

The success of women like Pam Flaherty can validate similar impulses in others and inspire confidence in neglected skills. These successful women were able to develop their own styles. We can learn from their experiences and observe how they circumvented common problems. We can see where they found receptivity. Their strategies for achievement are instructive. These women were not afraid to move on in the search for more receptive environments; they went where they were wanted, and where they could work best.

There are many examples of women who found others to help them in their careers. And they were not reticent to use those contacts. Surgeon Marjorie Fine went to work for two male surgeons who specifically wanted to capitalize on having a female on their team. Like her, other women surveyed often connected with powerful individuals who acted as gatekeepers for them.

These successful women have invariably taken it upon themselves to learn the environment and then offer what it seemed was required and needed.

These women *promoted themselves.* One business executive claims a key to her success was "tooting her own horn." She also deliberately gave her bosses feedback on her successful decisions.

Successful women with whom we talked have also *educated institutions* in ways to deal with them. When one executive sensed that men were uncomfortable, particularly when they were traveling with her, she *told* them, "Look—this is how best to deal with me." She informed the organization of her needs and wants and helped it to be receptive to her different voice. One executive invited uncomfortable men to join her in a drink so that she could explain herself and talk about how to deal with a woman executive.

These women's stories are full of hours spent voluntarily educating themselves and their environment. One television newscaster worked as a volunteer to learn the news. Her volunteer work led to a permanent broadcasting position.

Women who have succeeded in their careers have usually used their own unique skills and perspectives to good advantage. One businesswoman's position of trusted secretary to the owner of her company gave her access to information unavailable to others in the organization, including the owner's brother. She was able to capitalize on that information when the owner died.

All the women in this study had a *clear vision* of what they wanted from their organizations.

What does the experience of these successful women tell us about the receptivity of the institutions in which they worked? Where and why did these women prevail? What can we point to in our culture that encourages receptivity?

What particular institutions have been most receptive to women and why? Institutions that appear to be "women-friendly," that is, most receptive and responsive are:

1. Those that *need* women or the skills and sensitivities women have to offer. Some of these institutions have been mandated to hire women, some have inherited women, and some have had to select women because they comprised a significant percentage of the available pool of workers.

2. Organizations that are able to *see* issues impacting women clearly. These have consequently responded to those issues.

3. Organizations in which particular women are clearly visible.

One woman who has benefited by this new business climate is Debbie Smith, who is a Vice President of Xerox Corporation. She was married at twenty to a man with whom she had attended high school. They attended separate colleges and, upon graduation, looked for a city in New York state in which to relocate, since he had passed the New York bar exam. They selected Rochester because it seemed a good place to raise a family. Debbie feels it was a particularly good decision because she has found excellent child care and other services, and the commuting time is minimal. This had made it easier to attend school functions and conferences during the day and return to work quickly.

Today, she supervises eight hundred people and controls a budget of over $100 million.

"I am not the kind of person who could stay home, and not the kind of person who could be childless. I can get by with two to five hours' sleep. When the kids are home, I like to be with them. I get home about 6:15 p.m. and have dinner. After the children go to bed, I try to spend some time with my husband. When he goes to bed about 12:30 a.m., I go downstairs and work." She laughed, "The only time I have to do my nails is 3:00 a.m.

"There is a positive thing about my traveling. When I'm not home, my husband is with the children. There is a bonding between the three of them. He is closer to them when I'm not there. A lot of times I have called from work to say I have to stay another hour, or I have to suddenly go out of town, and it's not a problem.

"The problem is there is not enough time to do all the things I want to do. I am also active in the community and would like more time to devote to the boards on which I serve. There's almost no personal time.

"My job atmosphere is very supportive. Xerox has a pre-tax deduction which reimburses you for child care expenses. It also has an active child care referral service for permanent help. Additionally, they search out help in new communities."

On commenting about work/family problems for women who want to work in big organizations, Debbie says, "The problems are problems that would be similar for men as well—the need to balance work and family. Job sharing and part-time options are not possible in executive positions, since there is no way to effectively split the responsibilities. And to do the job well, it's a lot more than an '8 to 5' commitment."

She gave these tips to those who want to combine high pressured work and family demands: "Get good help and use it. Delegate at the office and home. You have to be very organized. Make the most of every moment. I have my secretary open the mail, and, if I have five minutes between meetings—five minutes dead time—I handle some paperwork.

"Know your priorities. In my case, the family comes first, if at all possible. If you know your priorities, you know what you are going to do about the inevitable conflicts that arise.

"I'm lucky to have a tremendous amount of energy. I've taken the red eye across the country to have lunch with my kids or attend a school function. Not everyone has the physical stamina or the desire to balance things this way. Nor do I, all the time. There are days that are tough, and times when conflicts force unpleasant and very difficult decisions. Fortunately, they are not frequent, and the rewards are *very* high. What makes you successful as a manager in business, also makes you successful as a mother. Handling multiple priorities and role conflicts is part of the balancing, and wouldn't do it any other way."

Positive Views of Corporate Life for Women

It is important to present a balanced picture that reflects the range of opinions in diverse corporations. More than half of our respondents felt that the retention of women in their firms was not a significant problem, and that there were no major issues impacting the retention of women as opposed to men.

There was substantial feeling, however, that education and time would remedy a large part of the situation. One woman dismissed the issue by saying, "People change to be more like the firm with time, but the firm also changes to become more like the *people*—that is, it incorporates women."

Opportunities for Women

Although all these women have had some gender-related incidents, they don't dwell on them. One woman said, "I don't understand all the fuss. I come from a small town where women don't go *anywhere*. The acceptance of women is so much better here (in an urban firm)." Many women with whom we talked were pleased with what they perceived to be a new meritocracy, with rewards reflecting work quality rather than factors such as gender, race, or prior connections. Many expressed their view that people in their firms are promoted for doing good work.

Of course, these are the women who have made it to the top despite all obstacles, and they tend to reflect confidence and optimism.

Corporate Success Strategies

There are now two female partners in one of the major metropolitan accounting offices. The women in the top ranks have distinctly different rhetoric than the women still in the lower levels of the organization. There also were significant differences between the consulting, tax and accounting departments. Obviously, the receptivity to women was influenced by the stamp of the managing partner in the different departments—some were more welcoming than others. Also, the nature and requirements of the work differed among departments.

What can be learned from women who succeed and stay with the same firm? What do they perceive as the factors that most contribute to their success? Here are our findings:

1. Confidence in their own style.
2. Active, rather than passive, management of their career.
3. Good work and even extra work.
4. Acceptance and learning about the environment.
5. Inviting and using constructive criticism.
6. Working around discrimination.

Both corporate organizations and other aspiring women could profit from listening carefully to the women who have succeeded. Others can learn what they value and have found effective.

Confidence in Strengths

Women have unique styles, and it is important to assess and value the things they do best and most comfortably. A woman manager says, "I'm really good with people. I get a lot of cooperation and willingness to help. My people know I'm concerned about them. I spend more time talking to the staff and telling them what I expect of them and what I am going to be doing. A lot of staff people come talk to me."

Another says, "I listen and get along well with people, so they tell me a lot. I'm their friend." Another woman states, "It is a question of the partner getting used to you. They have to see you are comfortable and confident. I haven't gotten any feeling I have to act like a man." Still another says, "I have a good business sense and good intuition. I am lucky in having a partner taking an interest in me." Another woman added, "I am goal-oriented and organized. I am good at salesmanship. I have clear, distinct communication which instills confidence in clients."

Active Management of One's Own Career

One successful woman said, "You have to watch out for yourself and promote yourself. You have to push. I said no way to the first schedule I was offered. I ask for what I want. I never look at myself negatively. I am aggressive and go after what I want." Other women offered *"Four times I went in and asked to get assignments on cases I didn't know anything about, but wanted to learn,"* and "I say let people know what you want. You have to know more than one person. That makes me more visible. I develop a personal relationship with partners and managers."

Do Good Work

Women are generally impressed that quality work speaks for itself and rely on strategies that employ excellence. "I do good work and let that be my trumpet."

"If they see you doing work at the next level, they will view you in that position. I see it as an opportunity to work at the next level up rather than as doing work I am not getting paid for. Management thinks of you as able to do that work when the next promotion comes along."

Another woman adds, "You have to act excited about grunt work. I was the only woman on a job with fifteen men. I was asked to do the secretarial work, but I did it and made sure my other work was good. I got angry at home, but joked with the manager about it, while still letting him know my feelings. He said he gave it to me because he thought I was the most responsible." One woman reflected that she was given a couple of assignments that looked bad, but she bore down and did good jobs, and they turned around into stimulating projects.

Accepting and Learning about the Environment

Successful women who rise in the current corporate environment don't waste their energies by futile fighting. Instead, they apply more energy to strategy or work: "I played college sports and it teaches you to blend in. You realize nobody wants you on a team if you're not a good player. If eight out of ten are men, you have to blend in."

One woman said, "I have taken their criteria and goals and roles and accepted them as my own. My willingness to sell out makes me *not* difficult. Then they don't have to treat me differently." But, she adds, she would not have sold out if the firm's goals had not been compatible with her own. Another said, "I try to be more casual about problem solving. I'm not so frenzied. If something blows up, I try to handle it. I can be serious." "I learn my strategies by *listening* to other people's *complaints*. Women need to watch men and women to find a style that works and fits," added another woman.

Inviting and Using Constructive Criticism

"I ask for feedback; I am not shy." As one woman describes it, "You try to learn from criticism. A senior executive chastized me and it hurt, but I tried to take it constructively. I felt at the time, 'Why don't you quit picking on me?' but you have to take it and change. You have to take criticism, and, rather than be devastated emotionally, figure it is a constructive lesson."

Working Around Discrimination

These successful women have dealt with sex discrimination in a variety of ways: some ignore it; some joke about it; some call men on it; some say it's the discriminator's problem; and others move around it.

Their responses are as varied as their personalities:

"I never really thought about giving in to it. The stumbling block is thinking it is impossible for women to succeed. But, if you look around, we really have a baby boom in this office."

"You have to figure out the female issue on a one-to-one basis. One fifty-year-old man took three months to get comfortable with me. I persisted and he accepts me now. There are pros and cons to being a woman and you must make it work for, not against, you."

"After seven years' experience, I have already gone through the militant stage. Instead of getting huffy, I turn it around. There are differences; they can be overcome."

"You can't be prepared to find prejudice around every corner or you will. Ignore it, and focus on proving your skills. Keep on moving forward."

"You can't take it fatally. I don't think a lot about women's issues. I don't act or dress especially femininely. I am aware that I change my voice when I go home. But, at work, I enjoy the colorful language. I progress despite any barriers."

"I was never a believer in politics, and, if I really was, I'd be gone. I would have spoken up and said these people are out to lunch. I wouldn't sit around and be discriminated against. Some women sit back and think it is a man's world, but it's not, and women can play the same game."

CHAPTER EIGHT

ALTERNATIVE WORKSTYLES

"Raising four little girls is a lot more work than running a business. It is the hardest thing I've ever done. Business is easy compared to my family. But I handle it by totally integrating the two."
Debbie Fields
—CEO

Debbie Fields is the young, attractive CEO of a multimillion dollar cookie company. She is also the mother of four small girls. Her integration of family and business offers one of the most inspiring examples of new work patterns and priorities. Visitors to her office have to step over her children's toys and around playpens and high chairs to get to her desk. When she travels, her children go with her. "Only when I am a successful Mom can I be a successful businesswoman," she states emphatically. Debbie admits that lots of planning is involved. In addition to her business schedule, she plans fun experiences for her children. While she works in one of her stores, she arranges for them to go to the zoo or other child-oriented activities.

When Debbie travels to one of her one hundred and eighty-five stores around the country, she is usually accompanied by her husband, Randy, a successful economic consultant.

Debbie says, "I am of the philosophy that you can do everything. Most people think you can't, but you just have to be well organized. For example, I don't go out to business dinners. If we have after hour business meetings, visitors meet at our house at the end of the day. They arrive attired in three-piece suits. But when it's 'Could you help hold the baby,' and 'Pick up some towels for spilled milk,' their facades disappear and they feel at home. I think it is important to know with whom you are doing business. A lot of bankers have had my spaghetti dinners on disposable plates."

Heading her own organization, Debbie Fields is, of course, in a position to set the standards, even if they are unconventional. Being a young executive and conducting meetings in your office while your children are crawling on the floor or inviting bankers to dispense their loans over spilled milk is not an option for everyone.

Nevertheless, Debbie earned the right to operate as a maverick. How?

"By making customers smile." Debbie speaks rapidly and enthusiastically, sounding like a cheerleader for her home team. Her rhetoric is somewhere between inspiring and exhausting. "Dreams and vision. It is having an unbelievable product and standing behind it, believing in it, and having total quality. I believe 'good enough' never is."

To Debbie, buying a cookie is not just a transaction; it should be more like a total experience. She creates that atmosphere by supporting customers. At her first store, she knew all the customers by name. When they stopped in for their favorite cookie, she knew exactly the type they wanted.

Described by her husband, Debbie is feminine and humanistic, but clear on the direction of her cookie empire. There are certain things that are not negotiable, but she is open to ideas that can improve the company.

When asked about any differences in her style attributable to femininity, she smiled. For comparison, she used the man she knows best, her husband. They are totally different in the way they approach the business. "I created it because I love it," she says, "I will not develop a product for a price. I start with quality and then adjust the price accordingly." But her businessman husband has, on occasion, tried to encourage her to be more cost effective.

Debbie learned early if she wanted anything in life she would have to work very hard for it. The whole family is tough and strong. Her father was a welder. Her mother stayed at home to raise five daughters, of which Debbie is the youngest. Early defeats were assuaged by someone with whom to share them: "Mom was always there to open the door and hug me. She was there with the words 'There is always tomorrow to do it right.' " Her folks helped her to learn to go back and try again.

"Good enough never is" remains her motto. Her success is due to great cookies made with care and quality, every minute, every day, three hundred sixty five days a year. Her own definition of success incorporates her success as a mother. She offers a new model of work life, of a CEO who designs her work around her family.

Such changes in the lifestyles and attitudes of successful younger women result in accompanying changes in work life. We have already explored some of the ingredients in these changes. Women in the work force are now routinely combining family and professional life. These women are concerned about balance, time and changing priorities.

They have found new ways to work—the technology of computer networking, for example, allows greater use of the home. And, there are new ways in which women *want* to work. The definitions of "success" and accomplishment have been altered by the need for success in multiple areas.

Many young, successful, married women with children are challenging the old concept of constantly striving for standard modes of achievement. Collectively, they have said, "I will seek satisfaction with varied kinds of success."

Interestingly, the most financially successful women rate themselves as least satisfied. One explanation is that being unsatisfied contributes to their ongoing success drive in the first place. As one advertising executive says, "I am complacent when things are going well." Success emerges from a striving nature. Satisfaction may remove some of the thrust that results in greater success—but not all.

However, the women with whom Ferguson spoke also are no longer satisfied with success as it has traditionally been defined. In the past, women have had little experience with the results of professional prosperity, since there have been few models. It is hard to gauge what new levels of success will mean to women and what the long term impact of a woman's success will be on her life and family.

One woman who has designed a workstyle accenting her mother role is Peggy Noonan, a former presidential speechwriter to Ronald Reagan and George Bush and a single mother. She has one son, Willie, who has just celebrated his third birthday. "I come from a lucky perspective. I am a writer and can work at home. That is the luckiest thing imaginable. Crocheters, artists and writers can stay at home, and it means that, even if I am working nine to five, my son knows that I am in the back room doing work. He knows that if he falls and hurts his head, he can come in and get a hug."

Peggy talked about her sister, Kathy, who is expecting her third child and is a working, stay-at-home mom. She says she experiences interesting problems because there are tensions with some of her friends who have to work and feel some resentment that Kathy stays at home. It sometimes makes Kathy feel defensive about a decision that women in the '50s made with profound ease. Now, stay-at-home mothers are often criticized.

Peggy is currently writing a novel, which she chose to do because of her son. She says if she wasn't a Mom she would be working at a television network or as a syndicated columnist. She has been separated from her husband since Willie was a year and a half and can't help thinking of it as a "broken home," but her son is a "great, happy, well-adjusted kid." She believes if she stays at home for two or three more years, her child will be well-launched. She believes "so much depends on the first five years. If they go well and are a success, the child will probably do all right in life." The decision to work on a novel at home is one she is "really comfortable with."

According to her, the day before she was interviewed went something like this:

"At 8:00 a.m. Willie comes into my bed and says 'hi.' He snuggles. I say, 'Give me four more minutes,' which he likes because it means he can put on cartoons and we doze together for about twenty minutes to a half hour. Then I ask if he wants waffles or yogurt; he chooses waffles. Gretta, the baby sitter, comes at 9:00 a.m. and gives him his bath."

Trudi asked if that switch goes smoothly.

"He likes her a lot, but he likes me better; I am his mother. When she comes in, he jumps on my lap and tells Gretta, 'you go away. I want mommy.' She says he is going to have his bath and he thinks of a million reasons why he doesn't need his bath, and, finally, I say, 'here, get him.' They go off to Willie's bath and that's when I have my cup of coffee and read *The New York Times*. When he gets out of the bath, we put him on the changing table and have a hug and kind of all talk together. Then Gretta dresses him and I get on the phone in the back room. A short while later, they stick their heads in and say they are going out. I call out, 'bye,' and watch as they go to the park. When they return, I hang out with them for lunch. Willie tells tales of the park—complete with story line and plot. At 1:00 p.m. I leave to give a speech at the Rockefeller Center Club— about thirty five minutes of talk and then questions and answers. I like it, but I am terrified of it. When it is over, it is a great relief. Someday, I want to get to the place where I can do it with delight.

"I return at three o'clock. Willie and Gretta are out with the neighbors and children. I make more work-related calls and business dates. At 5:00 p.m., Gretta leaves and I take Willie to see two gyms I'm considering joining. Later, we have dinner at home and then we do what we do most nights—go through the neighborhood seeing all our friends —the Haagen Dasz man, and the women who work at the Chinese restaurant. Bedtime for Willie is 8:15 p.m., but he likes me to lie down with him while he goes to sleep and it is more like nine o'clock before he closes his eyes. Then it's great; I have the rest of the night free."

After a little probing, it is discovered that on most nights she actually falls asleep with Willie and her great plans end with their slumber. Asked if she wanted more children, she answered, "I don't intend to remarry soon," but indicated that she would have more children if she married before she reached her forties.

Someone recently asked her if she was scared being a single mother, and she answered that she had never really thought about it. "I have a lot of family." Peggy's mother is living with her until the end of the summer, and her brother, an aspiring actor from Los Angeles who walked in during the interview, is also staying at her home. "It's delightful to have them. I am a lucky woman and I don't have most of the fears of the newly divorced." Money is not a problem due to her recent best-selling book. She has a satisfied, stimulating life.

In Peggy's opinion, the best thing corporations can do to help women is by having on-site day care. Then women can work productively and not have to worry about being unavailable for their children all day long. "They can be guilt free and pay their bills."

Trudi asked if she did her job differently as a woman and she replied, "Yes. My job really was listening to politicians. That certainly is connected to my femininity. Plus, I was not threatening. They knew I didn't want to run the campaign or be an ambassador. The male speech writers wanted to go into politics. I was lucky because Bush and Reagan like to talk to women. I think it was more fun for them. They were around men all the time; it was a break for them. I was just as ambitious as the guys, but for non-governmental things.

"As a woman, I think my book about the White

House was different than a man's would have been. A man's book would have been about 'What I did with power.' I took a broader perspective of what I did as a person."

Her tips to other women include: "Don't be guided by ideology in your choices about how you live; be guided by your gut and instinct and heart. Don't be embarrassed that you are guided by considerations of the well-being of others; someone has to be nicer.

"Don't get caught up in the proper role of women in the world, that self-generating modern ideology which says you damn well better be a professional—doctor, lawyer, speechwriter—and husbands and kids come after self-actualization. Because we know the kids are more important, not just for them, but because of what they do to *you.*

"You have to be guided by your own feelings of right and wrong."

When asked about her success, she replied, "I worked hard and had a romantic sense of the possibilities. I really believe that in America anyone can do anything—if you think that, it is more likely to be true."

New Work Patterns

Some women have to pioneer yet another role: that of changing their original work goals and creating work styles more in keeping with their family roles. Some women who have reached the pinnacles of one profession career seek success in another where a more balanced life style is possible. A dermatologist provides one example. Her concern was the excessive time spent learning one thing. Dermatology was her exclusive focus for years. She became tired of the same issues and wanted new, diverse stimuli in her life. So she made some unusual choices. Because the field of dermatology was overcrowded in Los Angeles, she and a friend opened a practice in a small oil and agricultural town in northern California. The town had a need for dermatologists. She could either make the two-hour drive or fly up in twenty minutes with her partner, who bought a small plane for this purpose. Flying time to the town was shorter than the road time experienced by most commuters in Los Angeles. Her new life style suited her perfectly. She worked two days a week at her dermatology practice. In those two days, she was able to use her skills, make a contribution, earn a sufficient income, and have a satisfying professional outlet.

The two-hour drive on Monday morning provided a pleasant transition from her other life in Los Angeles. When she arrived, she would put on her white outfit and work for two days with clear concentration. She returned home on Tuesday night, leaving her medical concerns behind, and was able to enjoy family time for the rest of the week. According to her, this was some of the best utilization of her talents she had ever had, and she loved it. After several years, with her children older and less needful of all her attention, however, she found the free time was simply being squandered and that she was not accomplishing much. She decided to make better use of this time and took up the study of photography.

Reflecting the same discipline that enabled her to become a doctor, she set up a systematic approach to photography, rather than leaving it to chance. She reserved Wednesday, the first of her free days, for shooting pictures; Thursday was for developing pictures in her lab. Friday was kept open for other chores and for herself.

The emerging picture is of a woman who rejected the usual thrust of career success for a bigger and better life. It is a portrait of a creative design that balances professional, economic, and personal needs. It is not the story of a mother forsaking work goals for her children, but of a woman searching for a rounded personal definition of both individual and family success.

Also, at different periods of their lives, married women who have achieved conventional success may choose to explore new pathways. For example, it is difficult to define the next step on a ladder for a woman like television journalist Jane Pauley, who is currently carving out her own new career path.

Another spokesperson for creating new work styles is a brilliant lawyer who had her first child after age thirty. Shortly thereafter, she won a coveted promotion to first female partner in an established Los Angeles law firm. At the time of her promotion, the firm agreed to allow her to work on a limited basis. Nine months after that, she resigned her partnership to work as a law clerk three days a week. Later, she found that she wanted to devote more time to mothering and had become increasingly dissatisfied with the "contentiousness" of her litigation practice.

As a child, she reported that she found neither role models nor career encouragement at home. Her mother didn't work; she was happy being a mother. Both her parents had a traditional aspiration for her to get married. They felt she should get a teaching credential in case she ever had any financial need.

Both in high school and in college, she describes herself as "lacking in confidence," although, in fact, she was very successful academically and had many friends. After college, she wanted to attend graduate school in Educational Psychology, but was getting pressured from her parents to get married. Before she left for graduate school, her high school and college boyfriend, who was then beginning law school in California, agreed to marry her.

She worked for two years in California in a secretarial position to help her husband through law school. She hated it and was miserable. Her husband encouraged her to apply to law school. She was scared, thinking law school would be hard, but "It turned out I was quite good at law school." Although she gained confidence in herself, her approach reflected her lack of total career commitment. In the fall of 1971, she was invited to join a legal publication, but turned down the position. "Declining was something a man might not do. I thought that it would be a pain in the neck. I didn't really regard myself as an aspiring career person. I even missed interviewing for summer jobs, and I went to Europe instead." She did stay in college for her third year at school while her husband worked in California.

After graduating second in her law school class, she got a job in Los Angeles at the law firm at which she was eventually made partner. "This firm had high hiring standards, but, once you were accepted, it was not particularly competitive, and it was assumed you would succeed."

At first, she worked enormously hard. Her relationship with her husband, which had always been uneven, began to crumble. "I might have spent more time at home if he had been available, but he was working very hard, too. We both worked six days a week. At the time, I didn't regard the hard work as a sacrifice." Eventually, she and her husband were divorced. Some time later, she married a partner in the law firm.

Four and one-half years into law practice, she and her new husband had their first child. The firm accomodated her with a six months leave of absense. Six months later, she was made partner. But she changed directions. She decided after practicing law successfully for five years, she had proven herself and "didn't have to be a hot-shot anymore." As a mother, she did not want the responsibility of being a law partner, handling cases that might require going out of town for weeks at a time with little control over the circumstances that had such an effect on her family relationships.

"I enjoy research and analysis. This is the part that I am good at. I was very good at law school and I have an ability to think and write, to take a fact situation and logically apply rules and analyze it systematically."

She is now forty-three years old. Her children are ages thirteen and nine, respectively. In the five years she worked in research, her role at the firm changed drastically. During that time, she developed an expertise in bankruptcy law and acted primarily as an expert in her field. She now uses her skills and interest in children doing *pro bono* work for county children's services.

In her case, she boldly rejected one pinnacle of her profession—a law partnership—in favor of searching out a successful new field which accomodated her role as wife and mother. She is a woman who has creatively restructured her own life and is happy with the results.

Job Sharing

Job-sharing and similar kinds of options are being explored in many organizations. School districts have written part-time standards and benefits into their contracts. Police departments are experimenting with job sharing. A nonprofit organization called "New Ways To Work" has been established in San Francisco to educate individuals and organizations about these issues.

A teacher/administrator, who had just had her second child and, somewhat grudgingly, was about to return to work, remarked that while union contracts provided for part-time work for teachers, there were no similar provisions for administrators. Upon learning about various unconventional working arrangements of successful professional women, she began to contact some of these women who had circumvented the normal expectations and established alternate patterns. She was seeking answers to questions that are becoming increasingly important: What does part-time mean in an administrative job where a person is employed for judgment and policy direction? How could that be shared or divided? What could be done? Did women sharing jobs end up working more than part-time? How were shared job arrangements integrated with the normal network? When she had gotten this information, she created a new kind of position for herself.

New Benefits

In many areas, policies have not caught up with changing realities. Many policies, regulations, and tax plans assume that the family still has a husband at work and a woman at home with the children. In fact, this is true only for a very small percentage of families in the United

States. If we want educated and well-trained women to have children in this society, we have to support the needs of those women and their husbands to take care of training, developing and educating those children.

Flex-time and four-day weeks are seen increasingly as accommodating not only traffic patterns, but family life patterns as well. Some firms have attempted to work out part-time arrangements for their female employees. Some have deliberately not standardized their maternity and part-time policies to remain flexible in individual needs and differing circumstances.

Forward-looking organizations are exploring new benefits for employees, including optional health coverage and shared medical benefits for husbands and wives. Some companies even have optional benefits allowing employees to choose child-care plans. These changing benefits and work patterns reflect changing realities.

Jet Propulsion Laboratories (JPL) is one of the innovative corporations in the United States that supports a child care facility for its employees. The facility is within eyesight of the company. JPL's Child Educational Center is totally tied to JPL's schedule in terms of hours and holidays. Employees are free to visit the facility during the day, and mothers can even come to nurse their children. "The benefits to employees are enormous and the cost so little," says director Eric Nelson. Parents are relieved to know their children are nearby.

JPL's Child Educational Center was launched in 1980, when the visionary JPL director created a Woman's Advisory Council for the female employees at JPL (who numbered 20%) and requested they provide him with a shopping list of desired benefits. He was concerned about addressing their particular needs and maximizing their career contribution.

The women listed on-site day-care as highly desirable and the director assigned the project to a deputy director whose daughter ran a child care center in Texas.

The start up was sponsored by a favorable company

loan. JPL continued tuition assistance, but the Center is only supported, not subsidized. The corporation provides services to the Center, such as janitorial, insurance, legal support, accounting assistance and supplies.

Since it is a company-initiated and company-sponsored program, great care was taken to establish a quality facility, specializing in a high ratio of loving adults to children. Other larger institutional child care programs have smaller adult to child rations, necessitating a systemized environment to maintain order. That regimentation can damage young children's creativity.

When we inquired why there were not more employer-sponsored centers, Nelson replied that it was less an issue of cost and more of adjusting to the radical social transformation of the American family and the partial transformation of the workplace. "It is an enormous challenge to fundamentally change family dynamics. We are standing at the axis of enormous change." Such a notion does not conform to the family pictures in which most corporate decision makers matured or the ones in which they raised their own children. One female JPL employee describes her great peace of mind knowing her child is close in case of emergencies, and in good hands. Her relief increases her concentration at work. Also, she feels it sends a potent signal to the women (and men) in the JPL organization that the company is concerned about their needs and committed to innovative solutions.

Policies about "nepotism" (i.e., employing a husband and wife in the same firm) are also rapidly changing. Most organizations have historically banned marriage between associates. But with women comprising almost half of the enrollment in many professional schools and entering the professions in increasing numbers, marriage between firm members is increasingly likely. Professionals who spend ten to twelve hours a day on the job have severely narrow social contacts, so limitations on office romances may be unrealistic. More and more organizations are experimenting with allowing employees to intermarry and are finding that it may work very well.

In one dramatic case, when a leading law firm prohibited a romantic liaison, one entire division simply moved to another, more receptive, firm.

New Business

Many of the successes in innovative work arrangements have taken place in relatively forward thinking businesses, such as new airlines, government and health care. One organization, the National Alliance of Homebased Business Women, was founded in 1980 to share information and address some common problems of the ever-increasing homebased businesses; things like home work laws and lack of credibility.

Independent Business

Many changes are occurring outside large organizations, in entrepreneurial situations that women have set up on their own. For instance, some women physicians are establishing offices near or in their homes. Others bring babies into work so that they can nurse. One dermatologist who owns her own practice has her live-in help spend the day at the office with the baby. She schedules twenty-minute nursing sessions between patient appointments. Although the nursing books say one has to be relaxed to nurse, she has found that she can rush in from her busy day and nurse quickly with no problems. She feels that because her life is normally so hectic, nursing on a tight schedule may be normal to her and her baby.

Alternative Work Life Explored

Many aspects of our social life underscore the need to further explore and understand alternative work styles. A quick survey of magazine shelves and book racks reveals the widespread interest in this issue. There is a magazine devoted to working mothers, books on how to balance the problems of work and family and a Presidential Council on Women and Work.

Alternative work styles may be explored by young workers, men and women alike. But, as Doctor Helen Blumin says, women have more need of the options. They have the possibility of being working mothers, so they have a greater sense of the need to examine alternate ways in which they can live their lives.

Corporations which educate themselves and are forward-thinking will best be able to anticipate needed innovative work patterns, to create environments that are more receptive to women and maximize the largest variety of human potential.

New Family Patterns

New family patterns are represented in the changing lifestyle of Carol Dinkins. As Deputy Attorney General, she was second in command to William French Smith in the Justice Department. She is a woman who is leading a life that is interesting and unusual. In the 1980s, she had major responsibility for the administration of 60,000 employees and a $3.5 billion budget and still managed to commute on weekends to Houston to be with her husband and two children. It was a demanding routine. But, she says, "It was not my favorite lifestyle, but it was just one of those things. I had to do it if I wanted to have the job. It was hard."

"I left my family in Texas, moving to Washington, D.C. in April 1981 to become Assistant Attorney General in charge of the Department's Land and Natural Resources Division.

"I had been introduced to Governor Clements of Texas to do environmental policy work for the state on a *pro bono* basis. Subsequently, he recommended me to President Reagan's transition team. My credentials were reviewed by the transition team, and I was selected on my merits. I started the job of Deputy Attorney General in

1984." During the period in which she held that post, her husband continued to live in Texas with the children.

"I can balance my professional life and family life because those are the only two things I do. It is workable because I don't do a lot of other things like entertaining or engaging in other public work."

Certainly a key to her success is that she decided early that she wanted to be a lawyer. "My dad was the only lawyer in a small town, Mathis, Texas, an agricultural town of 6,000. I liked what he did, which was read and write and meet people.

"When you grow up in a small town, you are always involved in lots of things. There were only fifty people in my senior class in high school and two hundred in the whole school. You don't have to be particularly good at something to try it. In order to have a choir or a band, they need everybody, even if you're not good. So that builds confidence. You get to have different experiences and opportunities. You also get support, people are interested in you. When you win anything—even a spelling bee—it gets on the front page of the local paper with a picture.

"Part of my success is due to the fact that I knew what I wanted to do and moved from one thing to the next. I've always been positioned in the right place.

"I met my husband as a freshman and married as a sophomore. We had our first baby girl before I entered law school and one right after.

"Upon graduation, I went to work for the Texas Law Institute of Coastal and Marine Resources. I deliberately chose that job rather than working in a firm because I didn't want to work that hard then, as I had two young children. Also there were not many women in law firms. This choice of the Institute seemed more appropriate at the time for a woman. Finally, I was curious about learning a new area of law which was just really emerging—environmental law. I did research, wrote and put on conferences.

"In 1973, I was recruited by the law firm of Vinson

& Elkins, who needed an environmental lawyer. I became the first woman partner in January, 1980.

"My personal style is fairly calm and pretty straight forward. I am not too focused on being a woman. But many people in business want to see women do well. Having been one of the first women in such a position of prominence is helpful. It is not a criteria for any job, but it brings attention; an effective woman is applauded. I don't think anything I do is particularly different from men, but, of course, I know and work with more men.

"There are few women my age who share the same background and are making the same kind of progress. Of course, I wouldn't have time to be with them, even if they did exist, mind you.

"Support comes from family and friends. It comes in the form of not expecting anyone to be superman. When you have a bad day, they are tolerant, and, when you do well, they are happy for you. But it isn't just blind luck. When I took a job with the law firm I knew who I was getting involved with. When I came for the interview with the Attorney General and Deputy Attorney General, I saw they were sterling men. I didn't just do it for the job, but the people.

"Times have changed so that now men, who would have been reluctant about women in the workplace, have daughters who want to go to law school, and that changes their attitudes.

"I've grown as I progressed in my success. I learned as opportunities came along. When I got out of high school, I had never been on an airplane. When I started work, I had never gotten a rental car or a boarding pass."

Carol's children are now eighteen and twenty-one and go to college. "So I now have more time to devote to business—go on boards of professional and related organizations."

She gives the following tips on the job: "Focus and understand priorities. Recognize you won't always be going at this particular clip and do things with the kids. Recognize things change from day to day and then the needs are different. You need to look for perspective at a ten to twenty-year period. You need to be organized, flexible, have good help and support at home and at work. During the years my children were growing up, my husband was sometimes called on to go to school functions and do car pooling, things he might not have done otherwise, but he didn't complain. Verbally and emotionally, he was supportive and encouraging.

"Self confidence helps. You have to be balanced. It is inevitable to worry. I keep coming back to the fact that if I stayed at home all the time, I would be difficult and unpleasant to deal with. At home, plan time with the kids. I have not turned down projects or cases, and I did fit it together. I did go to school functions and girl scouts, but I did get up at 4:00 o'clock in the morning. What I gave up is a lot of sleep."

CHAPTER NINE

PROBLEMS ON THE WORKFRONT

The problem of the '70s and '80s was getting women into organizations. The problem of the '90s is keeping them there."

—Jan C., Executive V.P.
Major Corporation

Though the women in our study succeeded despite discrimination, even successful professional women aren't immune to the effects of male chauvinism and the subtler forms of discrimination that exist in some work environments. Certainly the women in this study were not exceptions and, when prompted, many recalled situations in which they had been overlooked, ignored, and excluded, both willingly and accidentally, by their male counterparts. However, these women refused to allow such experiences to impede their progress toward success.

Still, a doctor recounted the experience she had trying to convince the head of her department that she could handle as many surgeries as her male colleagues. A woman executive recalled meeting people for the first time who seemed surprised the boss was female. A Hollywood director/producer told about the time she joined three movie executives for lunch at a pricey restaurant during a time when she was a "hot" property. As she stood with them waiting for a table, the maitre d' said, "Your reservation is for four. Do you want to wait for the other gentleman?" All she could do was point to herself and say, "I'm him."

There is no doubt that, at some point in their careers, being excluded had some impact on the ability of these women, as it has had on others, to perform their jobs and earn advancement. A *Wall Street Journal/* Gallup survey of seven hundred twenty-two successful women business executives indicated they felt their advancement was inhibited because they were excluded from male social activities—events where informal, but significant, business was conducted. Even among the highly successful professional women in this study, who represented a wide range of lifestyles and occupations, such customs and attitudes had occasionally inhibited their progress.

A major goal of our study was to identify obstacles women viewed as having affected success throughout their careers. To achieve our objective, each woman was asked to discuss all the impediments she experienced.

Few of those with whom we talked, however, emphasized the issues of favoritism or discrimination when they spoke of the problems they had encountered in their careers. In fact, although all acknowledged being aware of so-called "glass ceilings" and other exclusionary policies, they downplayed the significance of these obstacles in their own pursuits of success. As a group, they were upbeat and optimistic, and, therefore, not given to doubts or negativity. Also, they had arrived, and therefore felt they had overcome things that had given them earlier trouble. As far as they were concerned, the most important current barriers to their own future successes were the ones they carried in their own heads.

One firm's record

A recent study on retention rates of women in partnership done by Ms. Ferguson at one of the big eight accounting firms indicates that although the firm hires almost equal numbers of entry-level women and men, it does not retain women in the same numbers.

It is both a business and a social problem. Recruiting, hiring, training and promoting women is expensive.

Additionally, the nature of the accounting business is changing from its typically hierarchical format. There is less staff work and more consulting that depends on continuity of relationships. The old philosophy that used to support an "up or out" attitude is no longer cost-effective.

These big eight accounting firms generally represent the blue-blood organizations of the country. Their employees dress and act conservatively, since they represent the interests of conservative institutions. They have not been at the leading edge of organization change.

Today, however, these organizations are finding that half of the available workpool graduating from universities and graduate programs is female.

The first problem is that no one knows much about the preferences of working women, particularly working mothers. We all carry around stereotypes about what will or should happen, based on our own upbringings, values and experiences.

The top managements at several major firms felt increased exposure to problems of retention now that they are being forced by circumstances to make half of their new hires women. They measure the ability to retain these women against their own stereotypes. Lacking reliable guidelines, they fear the worst, thus launching an unfortunate cycle of self-fulfilling prophecy.

Here is what happened at another major firm:

One of the first women employed by the firm had been identified as a fast tracker. She had worked four years and had gotten rave reviews; the male partners were relieved to feel so positive about the potential of this woman. While employed, she married, with no adverse effects on her career. In her fourth year at the firm, she became pregnant. In the absence of any standardized pregnancy policies, she appealed to management to grant her a leave of absence, which they were happy to do. The firm wanted to offer flexibility and support to this valued employee. Her intention was to return to work after several months. However, she found herself wanting to stay home longer following the birth of her child. She and the firm found themselves going through endless negotiations trying to find a solution while they both wrestled with their ambivalence. As each side was postulating its limits, the other was trying to determine what other women would want to do. The specific needs of this individual woman and the firm were getting confused with the larger stereotypes about this unresolved dilemma. Both males and other women were watching avidly. As a result, expectations and prejudices were built up by members of the firm that were going to prescribe what all women having babies would do, since this woman was the first employee in this situation. The stereotypes in this instance were based not on malevolence, but simply on limited experience.

Fortunately, management at this firm was forward-thinking. Rather than making blanket assumptions about women in general, because of the desires of one particular employee, they set out to learn about the behavior and attitudes of the other women in their firm in an attempt to draw conclusions beyond their own hunches about retention of women.

They hired as an outside consultant one of our authors, Trudi Ferguson, to explore the retention rates of women into partnership to determine if there was a significant difference between the retention rates of men and women and, if so, why.

Prior to her collecting any data, they assumed that women quit the workforce more frequently than men; that they leave primarily to have children and to look after their families; and that women are not as serious about their careers.

The data confirmed that women do leave more frequently than their male colleagues. The biggest discrepancies between retention rates of men and women occur between the third and fourth years and between the seventh and eighth years—the years of standard promotions.

The women themselves tell us why. Contrary to the prevailing belief, they do not leave to take care of their families. They leave to take other jobs they describe as more predictable. They take positions where they may work just as hard, but they can count on certain regular hours and are able to make arrangements for dependable child care. These women are bright, well-trained and are in demand on the open market. What happens in the organizations to push these women out?

The organization is interested in the women who might stay, *but for* . . . what are the *but fors* in the organization and how are they related to the receptivity of the marketplace to women?

Factors Influencing Retention of Women into Partnership

The following specific observations were made during in-depth individual interviews with thirty-six professional women, including nine interviews with professional women who recently left one major firm. In addition, there were two group-interviews with a total of eighteen additional women, and seven male partners, all employed in major metropolitan offices.

The interviews focused on obstacles to retention and promotion of women into partnership. Although a feminine majority of 58% said there was no problem for women, the remaining 42% did identify environmental obstacles. These comments come from women still operating at the lower levels of the firm and are likely to represent a different view from the successful women described earlier.

General themes emerged as having an impact on a woman's remaining with the firm and are significant for other corporate environments, including hiring procedure, lack of female role models at the top, unclear career paths and potential, the exclusive "good old boys' club," conscious and unconscious attitudes, differences in ways men

and women work, work assignments, family considerations, and communication.

Hiring

Management has years of experience in hiring
males. They recognize masculine signs of aggressive, effective, professional behavior and commitment overtime.
Management has had much less experience hiring women
and it, generally, does not yet know what distinguishes female employees.

Women's Career Commitments

Professional women complain that management
"doesn't pick up commitment from women." Management
may have a tendency to rely on traditional female signals
like neatness and good looks—the "cheerleader" type—and
to pay less attention to women's "confidence in business
skills and maturity." Women managers report an instance
in which "a gorgeous blonde was given an offer," even
though two women managers involved in the interview felt
she was not an appropriate recruit. The recruiting process
might benefit from paying more attention to characteristics
in women that correlate with success.

Realistic Discussion of the Work Environment

Another problem seems to be an inadequate por-
trayal of life at corporate firms. "It would be better to paint
a more realistic picture. Both sides need to understand the
risks and sacrifices." New women recruits may not fully
understand the real demands that will be placed on their
work lives. Consequently, the discovery of these demands
might result in early defection. "When I interviewed, I
asked about travel. I was told I wouldn't travel more than
ten percent of the time. I left because that was not true,"
said one respondent.

Women's Roles in Interviews

Many women have been socialized to please and accommodate. They want the interview process to be pleasant, perhaps foregoing a thorough investigation. One manager stated, "Women tend to be a little less aggressive in the interview process and may not ferret out the true picture. They are interested in pleasing and feeling comfortable." Another says, "But women should know up front what they are getting into, because, if they can't deal with the pace, they probably are not going to like it."

Involving More Women Managers in Recruiting

Involving more women managers in the recruiting process might facilitate quality hiring. Such women would survive as role models and inspire confidence that the firm was aware of and receptive to women attaining top executive positions.

Role Models

The lack of role models at the top of the organization impacts aspiring women in two fundamental ways. First, it sends a message that "Women aren't staying around," for whatever reasons: they are not being promoted, they can't combine career and family, or there is "no carrot at the end of a long stick of dog work. It thins out at the top. The higher up, the slower we go. It's scary that there are no women partners. It's a crap shoot, and the main reason to put up with being a manager is because you want to be a partner."

Second, not having role models denies aspiring women the opportunity to learn the steps to success. "Nobody knows what you have to do to be a partner. We don't know what female partners look like. If I could see a woman partner, it would help me make up my mind." There are no gender models to establish a "good old girls' club," with sponsorship and information on how to develop and use skills, how to juggle a personal and professional life, and child care. The lack of women at the top inhibits a sense of camaraderie and rapport in which women might comfortably discuss husband and home. It denies support and friendship in higher levels. Specifically, women comment: "I don't see women with happy families who are CEOs or top vice presidents. The only women close to becoming top executives have sacrificed everything. We want some assurance there is room for good women who don't have to be superwomen."

"It's hard to be a pioneer," claims one woman in the group.

Career Path

Women express concern over the uncertainty of their potential career path. They suffer the normal insecurities surrounding career growth, compounded by the lack of role models.

Older women who start their careers later because of remaining at home to raise their children wonder if firms create top executives over the age of forty-five. Many women feel career growth and executive potential are not adequately discussed. For example, what does promotion involve? Are transfers necessary, and so on?

Good Old Boys' Club

Many of the traditional ways of doing business revolve around typical male traits—a hearty handshake, a few drinks, a round of golf, a water-skiing trip, and lunch or dinner in male company. There is an intimacy formed in these associations that fosters important communication. The exclusion of women denies women the social contacts that provide fun, friendship and visibility. It reduces the informal flow of business information, teaching, evaluating, planning and strategizing. Partners, executives and managers may feel more comfortable with men they know informally, and, therefore, they are more likely to bring them into future projects. Women say, "I noticed this phenomenon when I sought a promotion. Men receive slightly more attention. It is a kind of locker room information exchange that I'm not part of. When men are ready to enter executive status, the male he reports to starts to pay attention. They talk more about clients, different skills, and job assignments."

Attitudes Influencing Women

Women hear attitudes expressed by male colleagues that diminish their optimism and faith in career programs. They have heard negative comments about:

- Their combining career and family;

- The assumption that women will leave after having families;

- Women's lack of seriousness about their careers;

- The importance of women staying at home to raise children;

- Part-time work;

- Assumptions about perceived negative responses of clients;

- Lack of sensitivity to women as a natural part of the professional population;

- Stereotypes about women's lack of aggressiveness and toughness, off-color jokes and crude remarks about women, and harsh, "Marine-like" attitudes about the necessity of hard work.

Negative Attitudes about the Possibility of Women Combining Career and Family

Many women sense a lack of belief that career and family can successfully be combined. Yet the aspiring women in these interviews believe the combination works. They want to have career stability and progression. One of the two female partners interviewed from one major firm said that male colleagues repeatedly ask how she manages "all that." She advised aspiring women, "It makes you start to think that it is hard—babies, husband—and to question whether you can handle it. Don't let partners assume women can't handle both career and family. We should take a more positive approach. Let's help people through. Instead of assuming women are not returning [from pregnancy leave], assume they are. Help cover for them when they are gone. Help women see they can have families just as men can.

"It would be nice if the attitude of top executives was 'We want well-rounded people, and we were lucky to have wives to raise our kids'," one woman said, "Business has to realize families have to continue. It's just the law of the land."

The Assumption that Women Will Leave

"Management is afraid women are going to leave, so why should they make them an integral part of the operation." Management often has the stereotypical idea that women aren't reliable. One woman described a top executive who said he did not want a woman on a certain job. His reason was that the last two women on the job left. But, the woman said, "I think partners have a longer memory of women leaving, as the last three men that worked on that job also left." Another woman said, "I think they *expect* you to leave, and thus don't take you seriously."

Lack of Seriousness about Careers

One expectant mother was "demoralized" at her low client load during pregnancy. Another woman said, "I have a fear if I become pregnant, they wouldn't make me an executive. One vice president said they would, but I don't believe him." A woman protests, "I worked hard through high school and college to get straight A's, and I want a career." A woman who left responded, "I wanted a child, but there was no question in my mind I would continue to work." Several women remember their immediate supervisor asking, "Can you believe the audacity of her (an executive) having her second baby? She just had one." Women felt this indicated that the male executive felt that having a second child was incompatible with maintaining a serious career. Another male executive was quoted as saying it was "totally flighty" for a nursing mother/professional to bring her child and nanny to an out-of-town job.

Many women were concerned about management's attitude that new mothers aren't really serious about their careers. These women are worried that work assignments and developmental opportunities will be stymied. A woman with children said her superior thought she was working just to get out of the house. "He had the impression I'm not serious about my career. My real orientation is to be at work, not to come here to get out of the house." Another woman said she had a child and felt she had to work *harder* to show she was not going to leave. "You feel you're asking for something special and management resents it. But I went to work after I had one kid, and I know what it is like to stay home."

A woman reported frustration, feelings of isolation and lack of feedback. "I was overtired from work, and cried in a manager's office. They took some of the jobs away, but said it was a home life problem. That wasn't the problem." She saw this response as a dismissal of her legitimate work need. "There is a lingering mental attitude that if women work a lot of overtime, they can't get the job done and are out of control at home. If men work overtime, they are considered go getters. Sometimes management supports women outwardly, but inwardly they say women can't handle themselves."

Another woman in corporate life reported, "A male vice president patted himself on the back because he didn't call me at home when I was pregnant. He had the attitude that I was on *vacation.*" When another woman told her partner she was leaving, his response was, "Oh, I didn't know you were having another baby."

The Perception that Mother Should be at Home

Management's belief that women should be home raising children seeps through, and individual differences in values are not considered. A woman notes her superior's comment: "You're just raising a bunch of juvenile delinquents, and you should be at home." One woman left to take a controllership job, but her boss told everyone she left to have a family.

Problems with Part-time Work

Women who work part-time received mixed reactions ranging from support to resentment. A part-time worker was told by the scheduler, "If you are not really available, I'll give you work last, because I want people who are more available." The employee said, "Working part-time, I don't even show up on their statistics. They don't even know what I'm doing. It's no man's land. Colleagues hold a meeting and say, 'Well, you can come if you want.'" Co-workers of both sexes particularly seem to resent part-time status.

Perceived Negative Responses of Clients

"Management may be too cautious about a client's reservations regarding women. I've heard a male executive say, 'I don't want to put too many women on one job.' That shouldn't be a consideration. It isn't a consideration how many men are on one job." There also appear to be certain industries that are "safe" for women; hence women may become limited to those industries. Women described working more with banks and less in real estate. They also wondered if male executives could play a more active role in *educating* clients about women in the work force.

Lack of Sensitivity to Women as a Natural Part of the Professional Population

Women note attitudes that indicate a lack of sensitivity to women as a natural part of the professional population. These attitudes show up in conversation, as well as in practice. "At the new managers' meeting, I was aware of the obvious perception (on the part of the speakers) that all the audience was male. They don't think of any women being out there." Slides were used at this meeting that were significant to men, but offensive to women; one pictured a woman in a sexy bikini.

A woman said, "Things that weigh heavily on women's minds, like child care, some men take lightly." Casually scheduling meetings for 7:00 a.m. rather than during the normal work day fails to consider child care arrangements. Or unplanned overnight assignments reflect a lack of appreciation that babysitting costs are considerable.

Stereotypes about Women's Lack of Toughness

"Management is always thinking women are not going to take control and be assertive; rarely is that actually a problem. A woman has to go out and prove herself just like a man."

"The executive clique thinks there is one model for success—their own."

"Management wants women who act like men."

"It still bothers a partner when women cry."

"Women have a tendency to be more chatty and informal."

These comments come up in considerations of women for executive positions. But it doesn't impact their work quality. "Sometimes management says women are too quiet or shy."

Crude Gossip

Women don't appreciate crude gossiping by males about women or within earshot of women. "If they feel that way, how much respect can they have for women in general?" was the consensus of opinion found in our survey.

Harsh "Marine-like" Attitudes

Women are aware of some employers' attitudes that show insensitivity to a balanced personal life. Many women said attitudes should be more humane. "They could reduce the rhetoric about overtime: statements that employees should be reading fifteen hours of work on the weekends. Do they really mean it?" The motto 'Whatever it takes to get the job done' grates. Women say, "The climate may be the same for both men and women, but women's *interpretation* of it may be different. Women take it more seriously." One woman gave the example of her commitment to pick up her daughter who was returning from a long trip. She announced her obligation well in advance, but business prevailed. She ended up sending a messenger with $100 for cab fare. Several women noted rumors about one particular female employee who had to postpone her wedding three times to adjust to her work schedule. These reports were not complaints from the woman herself, but part of the rumor mill, the stories, and a symbol of how management feels about the personal side of women's lives.

"A lot of the attitude around here is 'just go handle it,' with no emotional support. The feeling that we are a disposable staff bothers me." A female manager who felt deficient in her skills at getting clients tried to talk with a vice president about how to do so. "He said, 'Just do it.' I said, 'I don't know how.' He said, 'You start with the B's. I start with the A's.' It *should* happen by selling work in my area *with* that area's head person."

Differences in the Ways Men and Women Work

Men and women often have different styles. Men talk about "aggressive" styles as the important determinants of success and the factor that most distinguishes men from women. Aggressive means a strong handshake, a loud voice, the gumption to confront and take risks.

Many women have a quiet, more conciliatory approach which asks polite questions leading to new thoughts. These women may be less confrontational, working toward consensus and compromise. They may work more on the basis of friendship and affiliation, but the time they take making friends often can be an effective business strategy.

The problem is that feminine styles are less traditional and less visible, and consequently may be *undervalued* by men and other women as well. It may not be seen as effective, and may not be rewarded by status and promotions in the organization.

Women see advantages in their natural styles which appear different from the traditional success model. One woman said, "I want to be smart and feminine." Women have been socialized to listen, to be affiliative, and to be sensitive to subtle clues. They may have a well-developed sense of intuition and be better able to pick up non-verbal clues. They may go to a client, listen, ask, cajole, and get good information. As a result of their people orientation, women may be especially good supervisors. One woman says, "Staff and clients confide in me, so partners and managers use me as a sounding board."

One woman describes her own different, yet effective, style: "My attitude toward clients is very maternal. I go into a situation to fix it up. I take care of peoples' books. I hold hands with the clients as they write checks. I'll address the envelope. Women are more likely to do it right. Men make more estimates, but I don't see men as more aggressive. Men brag." Men's success, however, may be more *visible*, either because of style or because of contacts.

Women discuss other differences in their styles. For example, some women are more disclosing as they work, and they tend to worry out loud. If a woman has a problem, she may say, "I'm worried I'm doing this wrong." That worry might cause her to actually collect more information, resulting in an end product that is equal or better. But what remains in management's mind is that the woman was indecisive or out of control.

Women may be accustomed to and need more support and nurturing. Thus, they may take criticism more personally. In an attempt to protect women, or avoid an unpleasant overreaction, men might cut out valuable sources of feedback.

Additionally, women may be less willing to make demands and say "no." Women might be a little less aggressive about setting limits. Consequently, they may take on more and more until they finally reach the breaking point which then appears inappropriately emotional. A woman who left her job said, "Women tend to work hard to try and please. They worked me harder the better I did."

Another woman said, "Men have more of a crisis mentality. It's like they are used to getting ready for the big game, and they are commended for working twenty-four hours straight."

"My hunch is women don't fight as hard," commented another woman, "They think someone is taking care of them, but they are not. Consequently, younger women may have had even more support in their earlier years because they are less able to set limits and are more easily channeled in work areas. If the first years don't provide good experience, they aren't wanted in the third year. Then women leave."

Another woman said that women don't push. Men do it all the time and "the squeaky wheel gets the oil. I need more response. Does anyone know what I'm doing? I need more constructive criticism. I feel isolated and it is a scary feeling."

Work Assignments

It was our conclusion that many of the above factors impact women's work assignments in one way or another despite the fact that the women in our survey managed to overcome such deterents. The intimacy developed in easy male affiliations can spill over into work assignments. A key factor in success can be an executive who mentors a key staff member. To date, men haven't felt as comfortable with women, but, as one woman says, "There is nothing controversial in being a mentor to a man."

Concern for the customer's comfort may also limit a woman's exposure. One woman said, "I've had great little jobs. But men seem to get bigger and better jobs."

The fact is that women seem naturally less aggressive about pushing for work assignments. Women want to feel that they are given responsibility, client and customer contact, and varied experience, and that they are brought into meetings. They want to feel assured they have equal development opportunities and that subtle comforts don't impede their career development.

Family Considerations

It was also our conclusion that retention of women professionals is impacted by what employers perceive to be the competing demands of family life. Although most women want to continue working, some employers are particularly difficult on married working women with children, making hours and travel inconvenient and presenting negative or insensitive attitudes.

Communication

Despite these women's overwhelming success records, a lack of communication in work situations can deprive women of a sense of involvement and friendship, denying them a relaxed atmosphere in which they can take more risks and do their best work.

The lack of communication may mean less feedback, both positive and negative. As one executive said, "If we all loosen up and get more relaxed, then women executives can get more informal feedback and perform at optimal levels."

Hidden Struggles

Our research indicates that many continued problems for married women with children, who seek high executive posts, arise not out of malevolence, but collective ignorance perpetuated by hiding the realities of women's lives. Successful women who have combined work and families must be vocal.

It is chancy to leave corporate change up to the benevolence of organizations. The women in this book had to fight individually—often private and costly battles—to prove their worths and establish power, so that they were able to negotiate top positions. Most didn't feel open to discuss their personal dramas directly. They privately fought for and found their individual formulas. Doing this alone is much more difficult, draining valuable energy with psychological costs. Individually, such women either made great personal sacrifices or commanded accommodations by their previously proven worths—often after incredible personal struggles.

Without their extraordinary individual efforts, many organizations—because of their own inertia—probably would not be accommodating women's needs. Those corporations which have responded to women's issues because they experienced recruiting or retention problems— or they have seen exceptional talent in women they want— are still in the minority.

If women wait to negotiate their own fates individually they often are already in weakened positions when they enter dialogues encumbered by pregnancy or fatigue or fear for whatever reason. These do not make for strong negotiating positions. The outcome then depends on the muscle of a particular woman and does not cause a change of policy for women in general.

CHAPTER TEN

OBSTACLES FROM WITHIN

"With my first job, I was shaking in my shoes, in awe of journalism and in awe of the younger people and their expertise."

Rebecca Sinkler
—Editor-in-Chief
The New York Times Book Review

The majority of the women interviewed said their biggest predicaments concern the energy it takes them to decide upon, define, clarify and monitor their own internal feelings.

Many, at times, agonize over interpreting the appropriateness of their own behavior, how to limit and control excessive work requirements, how to delineate their professional roles from personal roles, how to effectually deal with their children's requirements and how to handle the emotional strain of a complex life. They worry over the degree to which they should focus on their careers at the expense of other aspects of their lives. They grapple, sometimes very effectively, and, at others less so, with maintaining loving relationships with their mates and healthy relationships with their children.

Many answers to our questions were influenced by the way these women today defined success. Having largely realized their early professional ambitions, their present view of success was not the same as it would have been if they were younger or less accomplished. Success now meant more than just achieving a top position at work. It included a happy home life and satisfaction in pursuits out-side the office. Since these women had a multitude of de-mands for their attention, what they did not want to do was gain a high standard of living at the expense of a high stan-dard of life.

Obstacles Women Identified
As Impacting Their Careers

Balance Between Professional and Personal Life	35%
Personality Traits	28%
Job Related Barriers	22%
Financing Career	9%
Personal Problems	4%

Time and Balance

Carol Dinkins says she has not really turned down great projects or cases, nor did she give up going to school activities with her kids, including attending Girl Scout meetings. As she commented in an earlier chapter, "But I did get up at four o'clock in the morning and gave up a lot of sleep." Manager Sharon Flaherty described how she left meetings early to fly to a different city so she could arrive in Burbank to go to her children's school play. She went to great lengths to avoid having professional demands disrupt her personal life. Therefore, she sees the biggest obstacle in her life as not the lack of desire, commitment or opportu-nity, but *time.*

Gail Koff is a founding partner of Jacoby and Mey-ers, a law firm with offices in many cities. Gail is forty-five years old and describes herself as a "modified commuter." She lives and works in Manhattan running the business she founded. Her husband lives in upstate New York. He fre-quently comes into the city Tuesday night later and stays two nights and they are together in the country on the weekends. During the school year, her three children, eight, six and one, are with her during the week in the city and, during the summer, they spend most of the time in the country.

She met her husband when he lived there and "neither of us wanted to move. If we had asked, we never would have." Anyway, she says, "Why would you want to be together all the time? Having space works for us. It is fine for the kids. They have consistency and know we are coming and going."

Gail married "late" at thirty-three. "I wasn't able to do several things at once like working and committing to a relationship. I spent a lot of time and energy getting there. Then, having arrived, I was not happy. A whole other piece of me was not developed and not used and I was lonely. I had viewed men as coming over and taking over your life. Practically speaking, that kept me uninvolved.

"Interestingly, I got married and started my business simultaneously. I had done *pro bono* work and worked for legal services in the late sixties. I had gone into law thinking I would practice. I was interested in making law accessible to the average person and not intimidating people. The business started in California and I raised capital in the east after 1977 when lawyers could advertise. The idea was to provide affordable legal services to people. There was a market niche. We waited four years to have children. By then, the business was more established and there was some financial security. My husband is an entrepreneur, does architecture and real estate."

Reflecting on having her third child at forty-four, she said, "Friends thought I was crazy to want another child. My mother told me not to be greedy. But that is old thinking. I'm not that old. It was my easiest pregnancy."

However, she admits, "Having three kids is expensive. I can't complain. I have a terrific support system. I drive the kids to school then get to the office about 9 or 9:30 a.m. I try to be home early most nights. The kids need you around, but it's always a conflict between office, home and some kind of social life.

"Being your own boss is fabulous. Having enough

resources in life is immeasurably easier . . . like when I was pregnant I could call a car service. Still, you have to know your priorities. You can't do it all. I do adore the kids, but, at times, it's hard and taxing.

"It is important to have luck, a sense of humor, flexibility, follow your instincts and heart. My husband and I, before we got married, went to a therapist to get support for future stressful years. That is something that keeps the marriage on a solid footing. You have to make peace with your spouse. You both can't try to do everything. You can't get hysterical; if you try to be immaculately neat and completely organized, it just adds pressure. You have to go with the flow.

"I can't stand how short life seems. And I have all those people around me who need me. I go to sleep every night and hope I'll have good luck and my husband too. Everyday I get more and more aware of the necessity for it.

"I always want to work, but I would like to be working less. I'd like to get this business running smoothly, so I don't have to be a slave to all the peaks and valleys—but that's probably a dream."

Optimal balance for these women involves more than just juggling the conflicting demands of career and family. To these women, balance is portioning out the right amount of time and attention for a whole range of desires, responsibilities and interests. It is a matter of fulfilling the demands of motherhood, finding time for travel, cultivating friends, figuring out how to include opportunities for self-improvement and for simple relaxation. Many women expressed periods of doubt about their own abilities to "have it all." In such periods, they admitted they wondered whether they should "chuck it," move to the country, retire, etcetera. But everyone said, in the more balanced periods of their everyday lives, they felt they had made very good choices along the way about their lifestyles and their dual roles.

Appropriateness of Behavior

Women wrestled with the problem of defining the proper parameters of their on-the-job and at-home behavior. Some lawyers, for example, worried that the contentiousness and aggressiveness required of them in their roles as attorneys would adversely affect their conduct in a family setting, or even their general conception of the appropriateness of their behavior. This was true of women in other fields too.

Among the female executives, the lack of definitive models of behavior, for their type of mothering and working women, sometimes exacerbates their sense of going it alone. Many of these women confess sometimes to having feelings of being "confused." They feel people are scrutinizing what they do and how they act and that they will be criticized either for their mothering roles or their career competancy. An obstetrician described a recurring dream in which she is accused of failing to get her license. A producer had a repeated feeling that her friends would say, "Ahha, we caught you," when she tried to exercise her talent as a writer. A studio executive contemplated the power she had over budgets and staff and wondered how she, "a fat little kid from Massachusetts," deserved it.

Perhaps these feelings were the product of a natural insecurity because high achievers who are mothers have assumed unfamiliar new roles. Without suitable role models, it was difficult for these women to know what constitutes correct behavior in their family lives or in a professional setting. How do you judge your own suitability and performance? There is little social validation and understanding of what it means for a woman to assume professionally roles of power and authority while attempting to be a good mother at home. The fantasy of fraud may be related to the question of the propriety of women functioning in several significant roles. One example would be doctors telling people what to do with their bodies and then going home to be dutiful wives and mothers. Without the social reinforcement derived from custom and tradition, it was difficult for them to know how to act when they reached positions of authority and power in one role, but needed to be democratic in another.

It is these unanticipated "by-products" of success that some of these women think of while they attempt to determine how the natural consequences of their success, power and prestige can be integrated within their feminine, maternal personalities. When they were struggling for admission to the professional club, they had one set of problems. With the onset of achievement, they soon discovered they have another: living with the reactions people have to their multiple roles of power and prestige, plus motherhood. In the case of one woman, it became a theme in her life as a professional. A successful lawyer, she is the first woman to have been made a partner at one of the West Coast's largest and most prominent law firms. And she has been happily married for six years and is recently a mother. "I am a happy person," she says. She loves her work, not just for the intellectual challenge, but for the people she meets and works with on the job. She loves the social interaction, the respect, the money and the recognition that comes from a job well done. She also loves her rich and rewarding home life. But, sometimes, she feels pulled by the demands of performing well in both roles.

This woman says she has a tremendous desire to do good. "I want to make people happy. I look to other people for satisfaction. I do most things for the recognition. I want a pat on the back." She finds the adversary role, which a lawyer must assume to be effective, extremely difficult. At times, this even makes her feel sick. She says. "If I was willing to sacrifice a certain image of myself, certain ethical standards, I could be a better lawyer. But I think it's more important to be a good person than a good attorney."

She has been motivated in her career to please other people. She pleased her parents by getting good grades and her law colleagues by working obsessively. By virtue of her effort to please, she achieved a position of power as a partner in her firm. But that position is unfamiliar and uncomfortable. The power is distancing. She senses that although younger associates, especially women, look up to her, they feel removed. Her normal way of relating has been altered by her power, an unintended by-product of her effort to please.

In her career, she is having to adjust to having the power and status that comes when practicing law. She compensates by playing down her status so people will not think she is unapproachable. She feels her position conflicts with her desire for warm, supportive professional relationships.

She has had the backing and affection of many people in her life: her family, boyfriends, the man who became her husband, and colleagues at work. She never experienced any pronounced sexual discrimination. She has an image of herself as her own person, and never felt she was discouraged from doing things because she was female. As the older of two daughters born fourteen months apart, she was more aggressive, articulate and precocious. She remembers chatting away at dinner and monopolizing the conversation.

Her father was a physicist who loved her dearly. He, too, was very involved in his work but, as a child, she never really understood what it was. Neither he nor his wife ever discouraged her from tackling something she wanted to do and they never told her overtly what to do. Instead, they praised her when she did something that met with their approval.

She was popular and well-liked in high school. While she hadn't really contemplated becoming a lawyer, toward the end of her college undergraduate years, her boyfriend took the law boards, and he suggested she take them too. In her effort to please, she took the test, did very well, and was encouraged to apply to law school. Not only were the two of them accepted at one prestigious west coast school, she was accepted by an Ivy League college as well. Her boyfriend was good about the dilemma; he encouraged her to go to the Ivy League School—and she did.

There, she got a taste of hostility openly directed at her for being a woman. At this time, she also began a relationship with a neighbor and confidant, who eventually became her husband. This man offered her friendly advice during the dissolution of her relationship with the loyal boyfriend back on the west coast. When that task was completed, he asked her to marry him.

"I tried to make a rational decision about getting married," she says. "I thought it was an experience I didn't want to miss." Still, it was as much a matter of pleasing her parents as herself, and, even though she felt unsure at the beginning, their marriage has lasted over the years. "We are compatible, and we love each other more now than when we married. There is great security in knowing the other person is always there."

Her husband is a year older and earns slightly more money as a lawyer than she does. She thinks he always believed he was not only the smarter of the two, but a better attorney. If she asked him for advice, she felt his attitude was a bit condescending. At first, he was surprised when she did well, thinking it was luck. She believed him, because she didn't really have much confidence in her own abilities. However, little by little, she won cases and earned his respect. Now, he is totally supportive and reinforces her sense of competence. Despite his now positive opinion of her work, she feels he would continue to love her even if she wasn't successful at her work.

In her personal life, she has a very domestic side. She loves cooking and taking care of her home and child. Success, for her, is defined as being happy, enjoying what you do on a day-to-day basis and caring for the people in your life who love you. She says, "I don't want to be the first woman president. I am content to achieve being happy and secure as I go along."

Nevertheless, the biggest obstacle facing her now is to find a way to continue her close business relationships based on affection and be a loving mother and wife while holding onto her position of power and prestige as a law partner.

Obsessive Careerism

A number of women were concerned about spending an inordinate amount of time on their jobs. Julia Thomas has admitted that at one period in her life she was a workaholic, which contributed to her feeling inferior as a mother. Now that her daughter is grown and a successful fellow architect, she also frets that her desire and her husband's for leisure is restricted by her own acquiescence to the unrelenting demands of the job. One executive feels guilty that she never seemed to be able to reserve time for a family vacation, and even cancelled some holidays that she arranged.

Cherilyn Sheets is a dentist with a successful practice and earns a large yearly income. She is happily married to a man who, for the first years of their marriage, earned considerably less than she did. He deliberately chose a job for its flexible working hours, so that they could travel together, which they have done extensively during the marriage. Even so, her success and the professional demands placed on her were constricting. In spite of her "ideal" lifestyle, she began to feel the "classic female dilemma" : she was overcommitted.

"For a while," she remembers, "it was like we were on a rocket ship and just had to hold on." The demands of her practice, teaching and family were such that she had to change her working style. The event that most changed her routine and made her more interested in establishing a better balance in her life was the birth of her baby girl, making her realize she wanted to bring even more equilibrium into her life. Meanwhile, the change affected her husband's outlook in another way. He has become more ambitious.

Cherilyn was an only child, and has memories of being loved, protected, and encouraged. As a youngster, she was programed to think she could do anything she wanted. As far as her parents were concerned, she could be a professional, an executive or anything in between. Her mother, in spite of being a contented housewife, encouraged her to become financially independent as protection against the loss of her loved ones. Cherilyn's father, a dentist, trained her to be competitive and to survive by playing fast-paced card games.

At thirteen, given the parental authority, she decided she, too, would be a dentist. Her high school counselor suggested that it might be more realistic for her to consider becoming a dental hygienist. Instead, she decided to put in the extra effort and years required for a degree in dentistry. Her parents endorsed her decision, but warned her that people would test her capabilities. Even during her training, she encountered skepticism and patronizing attitudes among some men and women who considered her out of her league. While she was oblivious at first, after her naivete wore off, their insults stirred her competitiveness. She responded by completing her undergraduate work in only two years, and then proceeded directly to dental school.

She entered the University of Southern California at the age of nineteen, one of three women in a class of one hundred fifteen. They were the first females to graduate together at the school in fifty years, which added to the pressure she already felt. It eventually undermined her confidence. "When I graduated in 1968," says Cherilyn, "I felt shell-shocked."

She went directly into practice with her father. She had nightmares about taking her State Boards and doing badly. She couldn't help feeling that, as a woman, she was the exception, and, therefore, subject to extraordinary scrutiny. Still, she remained strong-willed and internally assertive, while, at the same time, tried to avoid being "obnoxious."

Eventually, Cherilyn joined a group called the American Association of Women Dentists, which gave her a chance to meet and be with other women in her profession and compare notes. At the same time, it helped her over-come her feelings of inadequacy. "The Association was a good thing for me," says Cherilyn. "It got me away from feeling things were so personal. I was able to talk to people who said, 'Here's what happened to me' and 'Here is how I handled a bad situation.' I also found that my experiences were very helpful to young women who were coming up behind me. Female monitoring was already beginning at this time in my life. I was being monitored by older profes-sionals and simultaneously mentoring those younger than me."

Through her contacts in the Association, Cherilyn made a number of close friends, and they all supported each other. As time went on, she continued her practice, but became increasingly active within the group. "I took it as a challenge to make the Association more active, and to extend the benefits to other women," she says. She was in-strumental in setting up advisory committees consisting of accomplished female dentists and top students, and work-shops on practical matters such as competing in the profes-sional job market. She even opened an information booth for women at the annual scientific session of the California Dental Association.

Because of her active participation in the Associa-tion, she earned recognition throughout the West Coast dental community and was eventually nominated to the Scientific Sessions Committee of the California Dental As-sociation. Their annual convention, which involves 30,000 participants, is one of the largest dental meetings in the country. It was an opportunity for her to be both creative and help shape the future of dentistry. This eventually led to her being the first woman General Chairman for both the California and the American Dental Association Meet-ings.

For ten years, she continued a very active role, and the demands on her time became more intense. She kept taking on more and more work because she felt like "there were legions of women behind me saying, 'Take it. A woman's never done this before.' "

Gradually, without really meaning to, she became a workaholic. Even though her routine was exciting and her responsibilities stimulating, she reached a point where she was tired and burned out on the overcommitment.

Then, ten years ago, at age thirty-six, Cherilyn had her first child, a daughter: "a total surprise." As a result, she modified her pace and changed priorities as were indicated by her new responsibilities. With a ten year old child now, a new phase has begun. This included an increase in her professional commitments in all new areas. She looks, acts and says she is happy with her life. What she really wants at this point is a little more play time for herself and family. She now aspires to achieve an ideal balance between her practice, her professional work, her friends, and her family. But Cherilyn still doesn't trust herself because "it is so ingrained in me to work hard. And I'm not really sure that perfect balance is even achievable—at least it is fun to try."

Rationally, Cherilyn knows she is successful. She is happy in her job and her marriage.

In other situations of trying to gratify a work/homelife goal, different modifications of tempo worked equally well. Justice Sandra Day O'Connor found she was stretched thin with volunteer work. With small children, she had taken leave from paid professional work. "It was hard to say 'no' to worthy things. When you are a professional, and seemingly available in the community, you are in demand. Part of my reason for going back to paid work —a job—was to put some order into my life."

Dr. Elizabeth Blalock, who was recently nominated for the presidency of her medical staff, ran for and won the position. "I didn't do it because I wanted the job. I really wanted the approval." She feels her children will be supportive, but she now thinks her commitment to the presidency would make it impossible to have a successful relationship with her new romantic interest, a filmmaker who is shooting a documentary in Africa. When asked why she felt bound, she replied that once she was given the responsibility—particularly as a woman—"You just have to do it. I couldn't let my colleagues down. It is my mindset from being a woman."

Congressman Barbara Boxer describes a similar situation. Her life in the late sixties included two small children and a frenzy of political activity—all taking place in her home. "When I wasn't working, I just kind of said, 'Oh, I can do it. I can do anything.' When I got the paid job, my life was actually less hectic."

Dr. Amy Roseman wanted, for her own sanity, to give up her obstetrical practice. "You want to do this without alienating people. I hate to say no and worry people won't like me."

Insecurities

The women in this study tend to view life as a whole, without making distinctions between work and personal life. When asked about inner problems, women spoke freely concerning those that emerged from their business positions and those in their personal life. For example, some mentioned worrying about the negative effect on their careers of their search for adequate time and satisfaction for their family lives. Many women had concerns about having time for themselves and their wife/husband relationship. Some worried that their status as skilled, professional women was intimidating or confusing to mothers and fathers of their children's friends. Several women said it was difficult to find friends who had similar goals and families. Some were concerned that they couldn't meet business entertainment needs because of family needs.

Losing friends along her career path was a serious problem for one business woman. She knew she had been on a fast track, but, still, one day she stopped to look around and asked herself, "Where are all the friends I grew up with?" It was a sad and compelling question for her.

The sense derived from these women is not one of their having to choose between being mothers and being professionals, but of their being caught in a modern predicament, participating in a contemporary drama that has no script.

Women's Issues: Pregnancy

Some women felt emotionally drained preparing for the role of motherhood. A young doctor described the trauma of working during her pregnancy. As soon as it was obvious she was expecting, many of her patients projected their own feelings about pregnancy onto her. They discussed their own experiences, their emotional associations with pregnancy, scary disappointments, all their feelings about it. She says, "It's nobody else's business, but it is everybody's business when you're a doctor and your stomach is sticking out. People feel they are allowed to comment on your condition all during the day."

Emotional Demands

A dentist, the mother of two boys, owns her own dental practice, sets her own hours, and makes a very good living. Her life has revolved around her need for independence—from a mean-spirited father, from a mother who left her with too much responsibility, from her family's economic situation, and from people in her early life's emotional demands. The irony is that she ended up in a very demanding profession. "Being a dentist is emotionally draining. People come to the dentist frightened. So, all day long, I am playing Mommy to the patients, and then I go home to be Mommy to my kids and husband. Even though my husband is supportive, for the most part a woman has to stroke her husband more emotionally. There is conflict with all these demands which nobody can tell you about. With children, sometimes you have more problems than you expect. You have to deal with them."

She sets her own schedule now. Five days a week, she works from 8 a.m. to 2:30 p.m. It wasn't always so.

After dental school, she practiced for three years in partnership with a team consisting of a father and daughter. Realizing that she needed to set her own hours, she established her own practice. "I saw a lot of dummies out there with their own business, and knew I was smarter, so I started on my own with a male partner." After a while, she realized she didn't want to work with him. Instead, she teamed up with a woman dentist in the building and they covered for each other in their off-hours and during vacations. It was also pleasant to have a female colleague with whom to consult, since practicing dentistry is isolating and lonely.

She defines success as knowing that what she does is right. In her case, it involves giving good dental care, charging reasonable rates, getting recognition from her peers, and enjoying her financial independence and family time. On the other hand, she says, "If I thought money was it, I would work longer hours and charge higher fees. But that doesn't feel comfortable, so I have to honor my convictions."

She perceived her special talent as a dentist as an ability to relate to people and their problems. It takes a sense of humor to deal with her patients' emotional ailments, along with taking care of their teeth. She says, "You don't want to make people feel they are acting in an unacceptable way."

Her need for freedom from the agendas of those around her made her go out and set things up on her own. For example, her mother, who worked as a teacher, relied on the children to do the housework. Hating it, she vowed that, no matter what the cost, she would have a career. She says she can't stand having to answer to anyone in financial matters or getting anyone's permission to spend money. She never wants to be in a position of helplessness if her husband "leaves or drops dead."

She is a cool, logical and self-contained woman, as well as tough, determined and practical. It was her mother who instilled an attitude of not caring too much what other people thought. Her goal from childhood was not popularity, but respect. She says that is more important than being well liked. Coming from a family in which her mother was the more central force and her father rather remote, she felt she needed to establish an independent existence away from home, so she married when she was twenty-one years old. Her marriage was one of the most important factors in her success. As far as she was concerned, it provided a "relief from all my emotional problems," and for the first time she felt continually secure. She told her husband when they married that she had no intention of staying home full time. That was fine with him. He gave her moral and financial support while she finished school.

Her decision to go to dental school was entirely calculated. She knew she wanted a career, so she assessed what she knew. She was good with her hands, and enjoyed activities such as sewing. Thus, she made a deliberate and logical decision to go to dental school. It was hard being the only woman in her class, but it was part of the struggle to assume the status of a professional working woman.

Now that she has a large practice, her biggest challenge is dealing with the emotional demands on her. Additionally, there are just not enough hours in the day to get everything done, especially providing enough attention to the children. "There is a conflict with all these demands," she acknowledges, "which nobody can tell you about.

For several years after dental school, she was the major family supporter. "I knew I couldn't take time off. I knew I had to produce a certain income." Now, her husband has his own successful mini-warehouse business, and he's earning five times her income. But his work is demanding and he typically spends only a few evenings a week at home. She says they are similar people, and share equally in their marriage, and rarely disagree. Her husband supports the idea of her working, and, for the most part, she feels her financial independence is one of the reasons their marriage is strong. Her income gives them both a sense of freedom, but the demands of their jobs make it difficult to satisfy all their desires.

"I have discovered the greatest antidote to aging is power. I'm into power. Why not? It's rejuvenating and exciting. Everyone in the state in dentistry knows my name." She is enjoying her term as president of the Board of Dental Examiners. "I am career oriented and have gotten a lot of satisfaction. I am now trying to give up controling my kids. I want to let my kids run their own life, for example, with grades. I used to spend time with kids doing their homework. Now I just provide the structure.

"I am now trying to do different things. Fun things. I've worked hard. This term as president is the culmination of my career. It's nice because I feel I can make a difference in the quality of dental care and standards for continuing education and influencing the dental exam so it is more relevant."

"The 1990s should be a time of moving women into power positions and having real peer relationships with men. Women have to develop those relationships one by one.

"I have discovered—much to my horror—that women's creativity and energy are often seen by men as not being a member of the team. We need to go beyond tokenism. Real power is energizing. You know more, and then want to know even more. It is not threatening to my husband. He had a big ego. I have never self-limited.

"For me, the point is not to try and change the world, but to get women to function better in the world."

In another section of this book, we talked about Elizabeth Blalock, former chief of Kaiser Permanente, who has been a single mother from the seventh month of her second pregnancy. She has not remarried or lived with anyone since. "My kids have turned out wonderfully. They are well behaved. It has been helpful for them to have a clear sense of what is expected and they had only *one* source saying what was expected. I raised my kids by 'benign neglect.' "

When asked by other full-time mothers what her kids were doing for their school projects, she hadn't the slightest idea—or the slightest guilt. She doesn't believe in giving up part of herself for the kids. For example, she is not supportive of the newest social phenomena of parents attending their children's soccer games. "All the parents do it. Kids don't need them there for every game. It gives the kids an inflated sense of themselves and a deflated sense of the parents' worth."

She was authoritative because she didn't have the time to go back and forth on issues with her children. She didn't sit down and do their homework with them. She had high expectations that they could work independently. When they asked for something and she said no, they did not ask a second time. If they continued, she gave them a raised eyebrow and said, "Have I ever changed my mind?" Her kids knew her time was limited and she'd say, "Let's not waste time fussing. I want to enjoy you."

She didn't feel tension between working and children, since working was not a choice—it was necessary. She was the sole support of her family. She experienced more trouble juggling boyfriends when there had to be a choice about being with them or her children.

Her entire work life has been at Kaiser Permanente. Eight years ago, she gave up her position as chief to move to Laguna Beach. She still feels good about the choice, which she made to provide her family with a better environment in which to live.

When she was interviewed, she claimed emphatically that, when her first child left home, she was going on a campaign to find a new mate, because "I don't plan to live alone." When the interview was finished two weeks later, she said, "I've found somebody. He is a film director who lives on a boat in Holland and travels extensively." They met on a blind date. He visited her in Laguna and has been there ever since.

When asked what institutions can do to help women, she replied, "They are always a day late and a dollar short." However, she declined a recent offer to serve on a Women's Issues Committee. "What are women's issues?" she asks with scorn. "Tell me one. Child care is not a woman's issue. Being a parent is not just a woman's issue."

Susan Estrich, who was the national campaign manager for the Michael Dukakis presidential campaign, is a woman who seems to have achieved balance in her life. Married at thirty-three, she deliberately waited until thirty-seven to have her first child. "I understood rightly it is hard enough to be committed to business goals without the additional burdens of children. It seemed my only realistic option. At twenty-four, I didn't want to have a baby. I waited to get married, but that choice was less conscious. Timing has a lot to do with it. I was not ready to meet or marry anyone in my twenties. Some of the men I went with then were as unready as me, and we kind of all knew that, so I was with one person two years, another a year, and so forth.

"I was busy making my way without mutual obligations—working twenty hours a day. In campaigns you have to be willing to move on five minutes notice. Wives and girlfriends are used to putting up with that, but my sense is that not many men would put up with it. In any event, I don't know many. "During this last (Dukakis) campaign, I was away for over a year. I came home to my house in Los Angeles exactly twice. Two nights in one year. Every other weekend, my husband came to Boston. I wouldn't want to live like that forever." Her husband is a Disney executive in writing and production.

"I did have in mind someday I would marry and be in one place. Getting married is an attitude, and I believe that you have to be willing to make changes. I am lucky to be married, but I am even luckier to be pregnant.

"I'm not living a frantic life. I've done that. I can miss a conference or board meeting without worrying people will forget my name. Teaching is ideal. For most of my life I did things that were very uncommon for women. Now, being pregnant is the most common thing women do; but it feels unique and exciting. It is more exciting than anything I've done.

"Until I became pregnant, I was commuting to Harvard. When I found out I was pregnant, I took a visiting position at the University of Southern California." Since she had exhausted her amount of leaves, Susan was forced to resign from Harvard, a move she found comparatively simple. "It was strikingly easy to do, something I thought would be devastating."

She reflected on a friend's comment that one doesn't want to live one's life on the male model. "Most careers are always a little disappointing, and I think many men discover—after devoting themselves almost exclusively to their careers—that their lives are a little disappointing. You know the old saying that no one on his deathbed ever thinks, I wish I'd spent more time at work."

Reflecting on single motherhood, she thinks it "would be difficult to do alone. But you realize being married—at least here is the guy who is half responsible."

On her time in the limelight and her temporary change of pace, she says, "I've lived through a year when I was a very important person. I worked until 2 a.m. and got up at 7 a.m. I worked seven days a week. I had my phone calls returned from all the important people and had my name in the paper every day. I've tasted that. There were parts I loved—and parts I didn't. I'm not so desperate for all that. I would feel far more deprived if I had all that—and I didn't have a child."

She enumerated the reasons for her success. "I pick my battles selectively and then I work twice as hard. I always expected the world was full of sexism, and I haven't been disappointed."

Her hope is that enough women will demand balance to get it. "The tone of the 'Mommy Track' is troubling. I don't buy that working mothers won't work as hard. Can we convince men and successful women to change stereotypes for us and for everybody? I think one way might be to say, 'Hey guys, by the way, some of you also might be interested in seeing your kids.' "

CHAPTER ELEVEN

PROBLEMS ON THE HOMEFRONT

"We all (women) have the same kinds of pressures in our personal lives, and my ability to be less prone to reactions than other mothers (based on constant demands of pressures of professional life) doesn't mean things bother me any less."
Yvonne Burke
—Congresswoman

In addition to organizational problems, there are personal problems which married mothers who work must solve in order to work and live more satisfactorily and effectively.

Some women talked of suffering at times from chronic emotional discomfort, a feeling that nags them like a persistent low grade fever. Sometimes, these women expend enormous amounts of energy deciding between conflicting demands. Should a women leave a conference on Wednesday afternoon for her child's school play? Should she leave her child with a new sitter to attend an important meeting? Should she ignore injunctions from her husband about her home roles?

Such thoughts are rarely voiced, yet they can exert such a powerful emotional pull over a woman's behavior that they dictate her actions on important occasions. With no acknowledgment or discussion, these dilemmas and their consequences are not only hidden from other women, but sometimes from the women themselves. There are problems of conflicting roles—mother, wife and worker. There are issues of marital care, child care and self care.

An executive offers insight by pointing to one of her biggest problems: that of internalizing everything. Her tendency is NOT to view things as the problems of others, e.g. her husband, her staff, her children, but to blame herself. She suffered when her eldest son continued to earn bad grades over a period of years. He was a difficult child and her immediate reaction was that it was her problem. She felt his poor performance was connected to her busy practice and her lack of mothering skills. However, after years of distress and reinforcement of the feelings of blame by specialists and psychologists, it was discovered that he had a learning disability.

She described the great relief, not only about her child but the relief about herself. And there was a note of anger at all the criticism she had borne.

Predicaments

Most short-term problems can be solved because they have ascertainable answers and can then be crossed off a list. However, the issues these women face are larger predicaments. They are situations that endure and persist. Marriage, children, work life are all situations that can not be "solved." Every woman surveyed expressed the same emotion in describing sometimes "being pulled." Others said, "The one thing you never have enough of is time." Some had feelings of having demands coming from all directions.

Marital Care

One professional talked of hitting a bumpy spot in her marriage when, at counseling, her husband discovered what he really wanted was a full time wife. She reminded him that she had told him early in their relationship that she wanted a career. Why now, years later, was he surprised? He admitted that was true, but he hadn't believed her; he thought such a desire would fade after they had children.

Elizabeth Blalock found her first husband supportive of her attending medical school. Initially he was proud of marrying a future doctor and felt it would keep her busy. When she actually became a doctor, his reaction was quite different. He didn't like the competing power that went with her position.

Artist and gallery owner Lita Albuquerque had much the same experience. Her first husband was completely supportive in the launching of her career. He, too, was an artist. But when she became very successful, he would say derogatorily, "I didn't know I had an 'art' wife."

Many women talked about the problems of making time for their mates. These included the problems of scheduling lunch "trysts" and Friday evening dinners or just time to get away together alone from the competing demands of the work world and family life.

These are the kinds of stresses that the demands of career plus family sometimes put on successful women's relationships with their husbands. At times, those stresses can make marriages falter.

Additionally, there are administrative care questions. Who does what and who is responsible? Many women say that, regardless of vocal support, the burden of household maintenance still falls on them.

One former woman legal partner laments, "It is easier for a man to adopt the idea of a working woman than to help with child care."

A recent study finds that cultural conceptions of childhood and parenting serve to reinforce traditional expectations that women alone bear responsibility for child-rearing and housework. These expectations may limit a working mother's power, structurally and interactionally. While mothers have joined the labor force in increasing numbers, men have not significantly assumed more child care and household work. Unless family responsibilities are more equally shared, it is unlikely that the status of working mothers will significantly change.

One story sheds light on the problems caused by this type of situation. One of those surveyed came home and heard her husband announce that he had to be out of town the next week on Thursday and Friday. She replied, "I have to go to Sacramento on exactly those two days."

Jennifer Lawson speaks of the problems when both parties move into highly demanding phases of their work at the same time, involving both in competing time periods.

Barbara Boxer acknowledged that her husband was usually supportive, but laughs at his heartfelt refrain (in the early sixties). "Sweetheart, you can do whatever you want just as long as it does not inconvenience our lives." For many years, Boxer spent enormous energy doing it all to preserve the marital expectations and screen the inconveniences.

Communications specialist Merrie Spaeth holds up her grandmother's refrain, "Marriage is a job." She talks of the stress of being the sole family support in a new business when her husband ran for Attorney General of Texas. Although she is clear about the fact they are partners, she talks of being scared and nervous when she bore the financial burden for their family alone.

Child Care

Although most successful women cultivate positive attitudes that sustain them when leaving their children, there is a constant high level of energy expended monitoring their care and their welfare.

Doctor Marjorie Fine says her children are fine, but she wonders what they would be like if things were different. She worries that her son may not have the social experiences developed by greater variety of exposure which was denied to him because of her busy schedule. She worries that he was forced into the computer field because that was the one thing he could easily do at home.

Congresswoman Burke discusses the pressure put on her young daughter. "She bore a lot of responsibility. She had to work things out for herself. But there is good and bad in the fact that you can't do it for them."

Both she and colleague Barbara Boxer did a lot of mothering by telephone. "The telephone can make you there. I always called her when she got home and she could always reach me."

Being physically separated from her daughter during her teen years was one of the hardest problems for Boxer. "If it had been two years later, it would have been perfect. It is hard enough dealing with a teenager in any case, but extremely difficult to have to do it long distance. I don't recommend it. Maybe I should have taken her with me to Washington, but I still had to come home every week. There were no good choices. And my husband had to deal with a teenager alone in her most difficult years." In fact, geographical separation from children was cited by several women as a difficult problem to solve.

Burke recalled the consequences of her own rule. "Whenever I am and whatever I am doing, interrupt me if it's the children." Once, during an important meeting with Casper Weinberger and other VIPs, a phone call came in. It was her daughter saying urgently, "Mom, Dad is being unfair and unreasonable." Her husband got on the other line to report, "I just can't deal with your daughter." Boxer crouched down, muffled the phone with her hand and dealt with it. It was not the first nor the last call dealing with normal daily family business from three thousand miles away.

"My first year in Congress I felt, at times, in utter chaos. It was a brand new and enormously difficult job and at the same time my daughter was three thousand miles away, also enduring a turbulent time." But her consolation was that "I knew all my friend's kids were going through the same things and they were living with their mothers. Even if I was home, she would still go through her teens."

However, for most successful working mothers,

their lack of being able to be with their kids because of working constantly is troublesome. They feel their children were denied some extracurricular activities because the parents weren't there to provide transportation and they didn't want to depend on and burden neighbors and friends with their chores.

Marcy Carsey talks about getting on a plane every other week to do her successful "Cosby" show in New York. Although she always invited her family to come along, they rarely took her up on it. Each week she got on the plane crying.

Barbara Corday describes dropping her daughter off at nursery school and crying as her daughter walked up the stairs with her little lunch box.

Anna Fisher had a distressing question. Even though her children had good care, she felt there was no replacement for a mother's love and watchful eye. In contemplating her first (and realistically dangerous) space flight, she thought, "what if something minor happens at home and my daughter's feelings get hurt? I would notice that and talk to her about it, but someone else, even a very good other person, might not."

Ellen Gordon's business is in Chicago, Her home, due to her husband's business and preference, is in New England. At the time she started working full time, three of her children were mostly grown, but her youngest still needed home care. Consequently Ellen took her daughter with her when she traveled. Realizing that her daughter's education was suffering, Ellen enrolled her in two schools, one in Chicago and one in New England. Although they were both private schools, they were very different. In one, for example, you could wear sneakers but not blue jeans. In the other, you could wear blue jeans and tennis shoes. In one school her daughter was told it was acceptable to count on your fingers if you forgot your multiplication tables. At the other school Ellen's daughter was reprimanded when she began to count on her fingers.

"It was hard," Ellen said. "Sometimes she would

miss events at one place or the other. She never did learn to spell, but she did learn the absurdity of many things and did get a broad perspective."

Marjorie Fine was asked about her husband's role when she was interning as a surgeon. "He wasn't happy, but it was kind of like he was saying, 'I can hold my breath underwater this long.'" At this time her husband was a new partner in a law firm. He was also trying to get ahead but he did work at home and never traveled. And, most important, he never said to her "don't do it."

Her worst problem occurred when she and her husband were on a two week vacation in Hawaii. Their children, ages nine and fourteen, were with them for the first week. After that, they returned home to be met by their grandmother who was to then take them to the waiting housekeeper. The worst scenario happened. The grandmother forgot and the housekeeper did not show up. Marjorie knew none of this as her husband kept telling her not to call, this was their vacation and things at home were fine. In fact, the kids gained independence, but it was not something she would want to recommend.

Current research attempts to shed light on these home life problems. There are numerous studies about the impact of working mothers on their children. One done in 1987 by Hari Venkartaramana evaluated the impact of professional women versus non-working women. "Compared to the housewives, the employed mother's parent-child interactions were concluded to be significantly more positive and effective.

In a study reported in the *Journal of Organizational Behavior* in 1988, Barling, Fullagar and Marchl-Single suggest, by measuring fifth and sixth graders, that children who had mothers whose employment status and employment commitment were not congruent were less attentive and more immature. In other words, if mothers worked hard at a job they liked, or if mothers didn't believe in working and stayed home, this resulted in better behavior, attention and maturity of their children. Whereas those mothers who really wanted to stay home but had to work, or were committed to work and didn't, had children who performed less well. The attitude and belief of the mother impacts upon the behavior of the child. The mother who is consistent may help her child adjust, whereas the mother who is inconsistent may translate those mixed, confused messages to her offspring.

Dr. Benjamin Spock, a leading pediatrician, theorizes that it is all right to be tough or lenient, as long as there is love, but the important thing is not to hesitate.

The study by Chase—Landsdale in the *Journal of Child Development* (1987) examined the relations between the resumption of employment of mothers of infants under six months and healthy attachment. Results indicate that early resumption of employment may not impede the development of secure mother attachment. But, oddly, a significantly higher proportion of insecure attachments to fathers occurred for sons in families where mothers worked. The fact that boys were more likely to be insecurely attached to both parents when the mother was employed suggests that some boys are vulnerable to this kind of psychological stress.

In 1985, still another study on child rearing attitudes of working and non-working mothers by Utpala Bose indicated that working mothers are less dominant, less aggressive and less suppressive in relation to their children when compared to non-working mothers.

Investigation of whether mothers' employment affected children's sex role orientation or attitudes toward household tasks found that adolescents of employed mothers had a more liberal sex-role orientation and attitude toward division of household tasks than adolescents of homemaker mothers.

The study by DeMeis, Hock and McBride, reported in *Developmental Psychology* (1986), emphasized the importance of a woman's preference for employment as opposed to actual employment status for understanding how women balance career and motherhood. Findings indicate that mothers who prefer to be employed have less anxiety about separation than those who preferred to remain at home and who were more strongly invested in the maternal role and less committed to jobs or careers. The interesting fact here is that employment preference, rather than employment status, had the greatest impact.

Investigations in 1985 by Easterbrooks and Goldberg—on the effects of early maternal employment on toddlers—show that maternal employment was not related to children's outcomes (security of attachment or problem solving behavior). Instead it was related to the amount of time mothers spent with their children and to childbearing attitudes and behavior.

In Robert Karen's 1960s *Atlantic Monthly* article, attachment theorist Mary Ainsworth suggested that the responsive mother provides a secure base. The infant needs to know that his primary caregiver is steady, dependable and there for him. Fortified with the knowledge of his mother's availability, the child is able to go forth and explore the world. Lacking it, he is insecure and his exploratory behavior is stunted.

Warm, sensitive care, Ainsworth insisted, does not create dependency; it liberates and enables autonomy. Physical contact is a good thing for a baby and a young child especially when it is wanted and sought. It doesn't spoil children. It doesn't make them clingy. It doesn't make them addicted to being helped.

For working mothers the day-care issue has been the most explosive. Attachment theorists tend to see full-time day care in the first year as risky. It is very hard to be a sensitively responsive mother if you are away from your child ten hours a day.

Other research indicates that a woman's choice for employment, the quality of her interaction with her child and giving or providing for responsive child care all assist healthy child development and negate negative effects of employment.

Some of the older women in this study have grown

children who have turned out to be, as Sandra Day O'Connor puts it, "fine young men and women." Their successful mothers and their successful development as children of working mothers offer hope that the problems on the homefront of providing nurturing care and good relationship can be successfully navigated by women who choose to work and have family lives.

There is also a body of research that speaks of factors which make women more or less comfortable with combining multiple roles. There is evidence that women's positive attitudes about self and work impact upon her ability to successfully combine roles. Evidence, reported by Pietromonaco, Manis and Frohardt-Lane in the 1986 *Psychology of Women Quarterly,* indicates that "highly autonomous" women feel freer to construct nontraditional roles for themselves and are more effective at combining successful marriage and motherhood.

Another study showed it is possible that employment status moderated the impact of family stress, although there was no difference between employed and nonemployed women in general physical well-being. This report by Neal Krause found that employment status reduced marital stress, but not stress resulting from child rearing. Conflicting husband-wife sex role expectations led to heightened symptoms of depression among housewifes, but not among working women.

The women in this study were high wage earners. Research found that women with a high family income more frequently assumed their roles by choice and reported more social support and fewer stressful emotions. Role choice, social support and stressful events predicted the amount of stress women experienced in their lives. Employment status, role choice and social support predicted role satisfaction.

Who does and who doesn't feel stress and how much and what influences that? This study investigated the differences between working women who felt more or less distress, stress and marital adjustment. Women who had "high" marital adjustment had lower levels of stress, employed a greater number of coping strategies and reported greater frequency of use of coping strategies than subjects in the low marital adjustment. According to the results, a happy marriage or good adjustment facilitates the reduction of stress.

Neal Krause's study focuses on women's belief about the appropriateness of their roles. This report indicated role conflict was more strongly associated with psychological distress than was job satisfaction, whereas the Pietromonaco, Manis and Frohardt-Lane study explored the possible negative and positive consequences of multiple social role, that is worker, partner, parent. The women in the Pietromonaco, Manis and Frohardt-Lane study had from one to five roles. It was found that all the women said they experienced some levels of stress but this was independent of the number of roles held. Higher self-esteem and greater job satisfaction were, interestingly, associated with holding more roles. However, neither marital nor parental satisfaction was consistently related to the number of roles held. Although many of the women in this study point to the stress, pulls and demands of multiple roles, women in the above study without partners and children said that NOT having them was equally as stressful.

How do women deal with stress of employment and family functioning? Much of the strain experienced by two paycheck families results from stereotypical sex role ideology that conflicts with changing realities. In other words, we are still using our own mothers and fathers as our own role models for parenting in a world vastly different from their generation. Women in our survey suggest that today's career-oriented mothers can find help in the form of assertiveness training to reduce guilt, increase self esteem and expand coping strategies, clarify expectations and communications skills training.

Findings by Suchet and Barling in the 1986 *Journal of Occupation Behavior* indicate that effective spouse support can moderate the negative aspects of inter-role conflict. Moreover, the more spouse support, the more satisfactory the marriage and the less the stress of conflicting multiple roles. Barnett and Baruch in a 1985 study suggested that it is not the fact of women working that causes anxiety. It is the role of being a parent, and not the role of being a paid worker, which causes stress for most women. The quality of the parent role was related to role conflict and anxiety. The better quality of relationship as parent, the less role conflict, role overhead and anxiety.

Jane Ritchie, in 1982, comparing the childrearing practices and attitudes of a group of working mothers and a group of full time mothers of four-year-olds, produced some interesting information. Mothers in paid employment differed in only one childrearing practice: working mothers placed greater emphasis on table manners. However, working mothers found their childrearing more pleasurable, their relationship with their children better, the children more likely to be happy and contented. Working mothers were rated warmer, higher in self-esteem, and less anxious about their childrearing. Husbands of working mothers were more likely and more willing to participate in child care and were rated as having a more affectionate relationship with their children.

Changing Gears

Another child care issue often mentioned is finding energy and tenderness for children at the end of a hectic day.

One of the biggest problems for Congresswoman Barbara Boxer is simply "clearing her head." All day long she deals with very difficult demands. Her work is pressured, constant and relentless. She finds it difficult to turn that off when she goes home. "My kids call me on that."

Supreme Court Justice O'Connor reflected about the possibility of over-controlling her kids when they were young. She was so worried about not letting her children suffer from her working and not letting them sit in front of television after school when she wasn't home, she structured their every minute. "As a result of working, I was probably more apt to tell our children what I thought they ought to do. Maybe that was an outgrowth of my profession. I have been a judge and legislator. I was used to making quick decisions. It may be my nature. I've done that a long time and it's hard to turn it off. My parents weren't as quick to come to judgmental positions with my decisions. My interventions with my children weren't always welcome. But I was so concerned about not having my kids drift around when they were not in school. There is much uncertainty in child rearing."

When asked if this had any negative impact on her children, she answered, "Well, you would have to ask them, but I think they are wonderful young men. Still, it may have."

The skills that serve these women so well in their careers—direction, control, quick judgment and decision making—may be hard to turn off. And they may be "unwelcomed" or inappropriate for their children, particularly as these children enter the teenage and early adult years.

Drug Crisis

Geraldine Ferraro's son was president of his high school class and captain of the soccer team when he entered a small, elite, ivy league college. He seemed the ideal personification of every mother's dream.

When Ferraro was nominated as the first woman candidate for Vice President of the United States, her son, along with the rest of her family, was thrust into the spotlight. By nature a shy boy, he found it difficult to adjust, but wrote his own speeches and made appearances.

After the campaign, the family tried to return to normal; Ferraro was in Hawaii when her husband called to say their son had been arrested for the sale of drugs.

"I felt like I had literally been hit by a two by four."

Later, she found out "Drugs apparently went on all the years at the college and they hid it. The information on date rape and drug usage was suppressed.

"I didn't suspect. Absolutely not."

Ferraro revealed that when she first saw her son after the arrest, "He sat down on the edge of the bed and said, 'My life is over,'" and she replied, "John, you're twenty-two. We're going to get through this thing." Afterward, she said, "We spent a lot of time with him. We went to a therapist."

But things were rough. Her son withdrew from college and, for a long while, "Nobody would touch him. There was no way he could get a job and we couldn't get him into a school." Finally, he began doing volunteer work in a program for troubled teenagers.

During this time, the president of Hunter College, who believed he deserved a second chance, intervened, and he was able to go back to school.

When the case came to trial, all but four months of the sentence was suspended since it was a first offense. (Although the prosecution and media sensationalized the case, due, Ferraro believes, to her prominence, he was arrested at a college party for selling 1/4 gram of cocaine to an undercover policewoman.) He was placed under house arrest. In addition, he was assigned two hundred fifty hours of community service and a $1,500 fine.

According to Ferraro, her son has since "made a positive out of a negative." He started and continues a successful pasta business and persisted in applying to law school until he was finally accepted.

Asked how she helped him cope, Ferraro commented, "We spent a lot of time with him. We really are genuine people and family is all important . . . The kids know we're there."

Ferraro said she did not feel guilt about working, and commented that her son's problem happened at college. "It would not have made any difference if I was working or not. What did matter was my notoriety and I have moments of doubt about that . . . but then, I look at history and think how long it might be until there is another woman candidate for a presidential office."

Guilt

SUBJECT'S EXPRESSED GUILT RE:
CHILDREN AND WORK

Amount of Guilt	Percentage of Women
No Guilt	50%
Low Guilt	31%
Medium Guilt	14%
High Guilt	5%

The majority of women said they had no guilt (fifty percent). Thirty-one percent felt low guilt and only five percent felt a lot. Some representative opinions were:

Arnold: "I don't think I would be a good full-time mother. I don't look at sacrifices I've made, but choices."

Carsey: "Every week I was producing the "Cosby Show" in New York for six years—with young children in Los Angeles—I got on the plane crying. But I noticed the kids were okay. I knew I had my engine running and, if I was a full time Mom, I would tend to hover—just like my Mom did to me. My working was good for them. I knew the time I did spend with them was more than most housewives."

An artist: "It's more difficult to leave the kids now (at fourteen and eleven and a half) than when they were small."

Evans: "I don't feel guilt. It is a waste of time. I believe in concentrating on what you are doing at the moment—to be there for each thing."

A business executive: "I never complain to my kids about work and travel, and they never complain to me. They see it as a natural part of life."

A dentist: "Guilt! Dump it! You have to be accepting of what is."

This study shows that some women also had private and persistent feelings of guilt about meeting their children's needs. Surgeon Marjorie Fine confessed that her guilt feelings still persist. "Of course, I have terrible guilt. I still wonder what the kids would have been like if I hadn't gone to medical school. However, they are *great.*"

One businesswoman said, "I have spent a lot of time at work. I have some guilt about not staying home with my son. He has lots of problems in school." A producer-director also has a similar share of guilt about leaving her child at home with a housekeeper. "Maybe kids are better off with mothers who stay home, but most creative women I know are both driven and torn."

Resources

Combining career and family has its advantages. In a study reported by *Resource: Careers "Report of the Dual Career Project,"* higher income was ranked as the most important advantage. Growth was ranked as the second, and more security and autonomy tied for third.

But the combination was also found to have its disadvantages. "There is too much to do" ranked first, couples do not have enough time together was listed second and not enough leisure time was third.

Self Care

FTC Regional Director Marcy Tiffany sums up the heavy demands managed by these women. She feels satisfied now that she is maintaining a satisfactory balance, but jokes that if one more demand is added to the burden, the whole equation will be thrown out of proportion.

Lita Albuquerque was willing to take time out of her work day rather than out of family time for a three mile run on the beach, meditation or other personal ventures because she found it necessary for her own energizing.

Barbara Boxer, who spends six hours twice weekly on bicoastal flights, lives in fear of getting sick. Barbara's assistant suggests that since she operates at one hundred and thirty percent of the energy expended by anyone else, it upsets her to get sick because she can only then operate at one hundred percent.

Self-care is important to Boxer in order for her to keep her energy level high. She exercises several times a week and actually makes it a part of her schedule.

One newspaper executive said she had to reschedule an interview because she wanted to keep the appointment she had made with her manicurist. She felt this, a very important hour for her, was one of the few in her schedule devoted totally to her own self-care.

Self-care for successful women often involves the issue of stress. One interesting question is whether the multiple roles required of these women actually develop and expand their energy allocations or whether there is a finite amount of energy that decreases with each increasing demand.

Nancy Evans says, "I am constantly called by women's magazines about having it all. That terminology is outmoded. That is a bad model. It is a media myth we can't foist on other women. Many times we are exhausted, but it is not said publicly. We don't say that Saturday all we want to do is stay in bed. What we do hear said is we wouldn't give it all up. Both are true."

Studying their lives leads to the belief that there is an energy expansion, but from our own experiences and the description of others, we think the area of greatest danger for successful working women is the area of self-care. Many women executives talk about taking exercise regularly, learning to change pace, having fun, taking more walks on the beach and putting the joy back into their lives.

This paradox is explained partially by the fact that successful women are stimulated by their role demands as well as, at times, burdened by them. Each woman in this survey had a real sense of being sometimes pulled between work and home life without enough time of their own. But they felt excited and rewarded by the varied aspects of their lives.

Problems sometimes lie in the form of personal help and situational help. Research gives us a useful tip. Linda Cox, in her 1985 dissertation, asserts women are best able to manage their stress when their perception about their coping resources is best. For example, women can increase their self care by controlling demands and events in their lives and/or by taking full advantage of family support such as a husband's help. But some research also indicates that it is not the actual control over the demands and events or the husband's help that is important, it is the perception of such help that is vital.

Research also explores what can be controlled by these resources. Self-care for women falls into two categories; managing stressful emotions and altering the problems causing distress.

We find examples of managing stressful emotions in the positive attitudes expressed by the women in this study. They responded with "I wouldn't be such a good mother if I was home full time" and "my kids learned independence" or "kids are happy when their mothers are happy."

Using the concept of altering the problem causing the distress, one executive fired two hundred out of two hundred and fifty people during a six-month period in her new, but failing, department. Jennifer Lawson told her MCP superior how to treat her and it worked. Women changed and rearranged the circumstances, helping themselves by making changes and solving the problem.

But perhaps the most interesting of all recent findings is that women help themselves most by helping others. Research shows that women who believed they were responsible for the well-being of others have fewer depressive symptoms. The reaching out, the expanded responsibility and the care, and even the sense of power also gives a perception of the ability to take care of oneself as well.

Self-care problems involve learning skills that take time. Many aspiring women despair before they have adequately learned or mastered these skills. Women in this study struggle, sometimes by themselves, to develop better coping strategies. They feel we all might benefit from more training around our own competencies, self esteem, time management and functional beliefs, as well as a sense of confidence and control over demands, social skills, health, energy and financial assets.

Women's Comments about Time For Themselves

Short: "I don't feel pulled. Some days I'm not feeling that great, but that's life."

O'Connor: "Working rather than staying at home with three small children and volunteering brought order. But it is a struggle to keep household and children going. They might have needed new shoes and clothing, but so did I." She plays tennis as often as possible and tries to have as many dinners with her husband as possible.

Fine: "I enjoy traveling and want to do less work, but it comes with the territory. You can't help it if a bus goes off the cliff and surgeries are needed. I'd like to spend more time away—learning to ski. We are going to get eight weeks a year for sabbatical leave."

Boxer: "I actually write my exercise down on my schedule and protect it. I exercise four or five times a week. Also I try and cluster my work so that I have periods where I can clear my mind. I would hate to do what my colleagues do and work Friday night and then again Saturday afternoon and then Sunday evening."

Tiffany: "I'm not that stressed now. I don't go to lunch, but I don't feel unduly stressed. The weekends are family time. At this point everything is great, but I feel if you add one more thing—like soccer—I'm over the edge. I feel guilty about being blessed." She describes sleeping late with the eight and six year olds, helping the two year olds to eat, and watching cartoons on Saturday mornings. She and her husband have opportunity to talk since they have trained their kids to accomodate it. But she also describes the end of some work days coming home at 6 p.m. and her husband is supposed to be home at 7:30 p.m. "I hate it when he gets home at 8:30 p.m. I'm tired and hungry and the kids have homework and that's a burden."

Savage: "I've worked hard and now I am going to try to do the fun things."

Sophie S.: "I remember coming home from work and reading to them (three kids), putting them to bed and fixing an industrial strength scotch and crying myself to sleep. I stayed at home on Saturday nights just in case my kids needed me at 10 p.m." Her notion now of a good life style would be to work and then have Friday night to herself . . . to do rollers or whatever, and then have romance Saturday to Sunday.

Flaherty: "I have to make time away from everybody who needs me. I have to fight my Protestant ethnic and do make one hour a week for myself or have a date with my husband."

One of the most successful doctors in our study tells this story of struggling and succeeding in combining personal and family life.

Amy Roseman, a gynecologist, feels her most significant obstacle was too much of a good thing—work.

At thirty-four, she earned over $100,000 in her first year working in private practice with two other female doctors. She attributes success to her "black box theory" that putting X (hard work) plus Y (perseverance) into a black box always equals Z (financial independence and socially useful skills). "If you were willing to work hard, which I was, there was very little chance of failure." But Amy was in conflict about her success, because "spending all the time and effort devoted to this accomplishment, I found I *loved* my work, but *hated* my life. I had been devoted exclusively to one thing."

Amy was the oldest child in her family, having one younger brother. "If my parents had a favorite, it was me." Her paternal grandfather was a dentist. Her father graduated from college to please his parents, but never completely achieved career satisfaction, working as a plumber.

Amy's mother was a housewife until Amy was in sixth grade, when financial shortages forced her to go to work as an elementary school library clerk. She felt trapped, both as a housewife and as a clerk, and returned to school when she was forty-three. Amy describes the relationship between her parents as "okay," but her mother was definitely in charge, in addition to doing all the domestic work. "My mother instilled in me the need for financial independence." Her father was not an easy person with whom to communicate.

As a child, Amy says, "I was always the tallest and fat." Her childhood was strict. "I was not able to do the things I wanted to do. I was frustrated. My mother was very compulsive; she did laundry daily. The bathroom had to be cleaned daily. I am also compulsive, but, for a while, I was a real mess. After I achieved what I wanted, I realized I could become a softer person. It is a big revelation to me now to find that I enjoy doing laundry."

Nevertheless, Amy felt that she got a special kind of encouragement from her family. "Both my parents and grandparents told me I could be anything I wanted to be. I was always encouraged. I knew it was totally unacceptable to be a beauty queen and wait for a man—or anyone else, for that matter—to make all the decisions. I was interested in medicine because I was interested in science. To see if I liked the work, I volunteered to work at Memorial Sloan Kettering Cancer Center in New York when I was fourteen. The hospital was a three-hour train ride each day. I worked all of one summer and was hired the following summer to work in patient research. I worked from age fourteen to nineteen. I made the decision to be a doctor when I was a freshman in college."

Amy finished college in three years and then went to New York Medical College for three years.

There were both good and bad images for Amy along the way. She met a brilliant female anesthesiologist who left a top position to live and work in a smaller town; one of her female professors was a workaholic; a male ra-

diology professor modeling the importance of broad thinking and self-teaching had put himself through a correspon-
dence course and high school, finally achieving a
scholarship.

After completing her residency, Amy joined a partnership with two women she met during her residency.
The senior partner was a role model because she understood what it was like to be a woman in medicine. She also
understood that Amy wanted a family. She boosted her
confidence and encouraged her. When Amy checked with
her on certain decisions, she was always supportive.

Amy worked constantly during her first fourteen
months in practice. Her partners counseled, "You have to
be better than all those men. You have to be perfect. Sometimes you have to overdo to prove you can do it." They all
worked enormously hard and drove themselves relent-
lessly, being on call to deliver babies every third night.

"The difficulty for me was that I was willing to give
up all other things for a limited time in school. But there
was no longer any advantage to being miserable. I was not
interested in having the busiest practice. Money is not my
number one priority. The work was satisfying, but it is not
all. I wanted a family, and I hadn't had time to pursue that.
I'd been too distracted; my job made it almost impossible
to take care of other responsibilities. When my father had a
heart attack, and my grandmother broke her hip, I didn't
have time to attend to them."

Men were not willing to deal with her schedule, and
she had no significant relationships for several years. "I
couldn't count on anyone or ask any favors, because I
couldn't reciprocate. I was only there one hundred percent
for this one thing [work], which took one hundred percent."

Amy says her top priority now is self-fulfillment,
and she is sure that job satisfaction alone cannot bring it.
The very thing she had been striving for all those years
"kept me from what I wanted. I saw the extreme choice as
either being an obnoxious doctor and giving up a life, or

giving up my profession. I woke up every day unhappy, and all the money in the world could not make it worth that."

Amy is dealing with the conflict. In the past few years, she married and had two children. She moved to a practice with one male doctor and several other females that emphasized a more regular gynecological practice. "I like the patients and they appreciate me. There is a need for a woman in the field. I like being a pioneer in the forefront."

Amy recognized the obstacle of excessive work and was able to begin restoring satisfaction in her life. She now says, "I am not happy yet, but I'm moving in that direction."

CHAPTER TWELVE

HOW-TO FOR INDIVIDUALS

"I run my office to prevent or limit interoffice stress. I try to do the same at home. If you don't, you just drown."

Amy Roseman
—Physician

From the women in this study, a number of consistent principles arise that can be of use to other aspiring women. Some were learned by successes and some were learned by failures. However, what becomes ultimately clear is that a wide variety of women have achieved satisfaction—both as professionals and as mothers.

Moreover, in scrutinizing their formulas, suggestions can be culled for other ambitious women who want to prosper in business while not sacrificing their desires for satisfying family lives.

Looking In a Mirror

Assess your strengths and weaknesses from the standpoints of self and family. It helps to understand both what you excel in and what you do not, and your family circumstances. What do you feel comfortable and uncomfortable doing? Concentrate on things you do well. You are the best judge of what fits your circumstances.

Suggestion: Begin by listing what you perceive as your personal strengths. Then list your personal weaknesses in the same way. Do the same for your family strengths and weaknesses. Success follows from recognizing and using the qualities and skills you possess.

My Strengths: My Weaknesses:

_____   _____

_____   _____

_____   _____

_____   _____

Family Strengths: Family Weaknesses:

_____   _____

_____   _____

_____   _____

_____   _____

Ask Others for Feedback

Don't get stuck in a vision formulated before your family life was established. Other people who share your life can help you define where you are today. Successful women with mates should develop a realistic and expanded picture of their persona, family situations and potential with them. Invite continuing feedback from others who are significant in your life.

How well this input is received, however, depends on your attitude. If comments are taken as personal criticisms, they can be hurtful and raise barriers. But if you can view negative feedback as a requisite learning process, it can be used to your advantage. It can be helpful to know what holds you back and propels you forward when dealing with your own family situation.

Many people spend large sums of money on lessons to improve their tennis games, their golf strokes and their financial investments, but neglect or resist feedback on the effectiveness of their own professional styles and how they accommodate their family needs.

Find Work You Love

Enjoying your job is a significant key to career success according to the women surveyed. This study and other research shows that women who love what they do, who feel they have a choice in what they do, feel less role conflict. Congresswoman Barbara Boxer dismissed the career for which she had been trained, that of stockbroker, because, in her opinion, at that time, the Vietnam War was wrong. When she is asked by aspiring women, "How do you get to be a Congresswoman?" she answers: "You don't aspire to be a Congresswoman, you follow the issues you deeply care about and see where they take you."

Suggestion: List the tasks you like doing. What issues do you care about? What gives you pleasure, stimulation, concentration, reinforcement, satisfaction? What do you look forward with enthusiasm to doing? How do you spend your spare time? Do you have hobbies or other leisure time activities?

Then list careers or jobs that emphasize those activities.

Find a Career for Which You Are Best Suited

Several women felt they were good at what they were doing, because they were well suited for the tasks. One who liked doing small handcraft and sewing as a child and young woman chose to be a surgeon. One newspaper executive was trained to be a teacher and did so enthusiastically for a number of years. But, being female without tenure during a professional glut did not bode well. She went back to school and got an MBA so that she would be qualified for a professional change into business. She felt that as a manager she could use her teaching expertise to motivate.

Focus on what you know and like. Take into consideration hobbies and leisure time interests. Use the knowledge you have acquired over the years.

Suggestion: List all the work and life experiences that have given you skill training—include volunteer and family activities. Through these experiences what skills have you developed? On a separate sheet of paper develop a list of careers that use those skills.

Use Your Unique Combinations of Experiences and Perspectives

You are you. Success depends on finding avenues to utilize your own unique style and perspectives. If you are assertive and boisterous, capitalize on that; if you are introverted and soft-spoken, draw on these unique qualities as assets. Successful women find their own edge and use it. Some women grew up with great privilege. Others didn't. Some had tragedies that propelled them, others had blessings.

Suggestion: List your unique talents and experiences. Assess them; they are among your greatest assets.

Remember: A Soft Touch Hits Hard

In the last Presidential election, George Bush was challenging his waspish, "wimpy" image, trying to convince the nation that he was tough enough to serve as President. But the words that won him votes and hearts were written by his *female* speechwriter, Peggy Noonan. She wrote about a kinder and gentler nation, she wrote about a thousand points of light, she wrote his moving speech about the NASA Challenger tragedy. The impact she made by using a caring focus was tough to beat. Many of the women with whom we talked felt that a soft feminine style can deliver a great punch.

For instance, said one, a sensitive, emphatic female lawyer may get further cross-examining a teary, scared witness than would the abrasive grilling of her male colleague.

Suggestion: Review and list the times you have succeeded by using a "feminine" approach, that is, sympathy, empathy, cooperation or sensitivity. Recognize that femininity can be a positive, not a negative, force in attaining success.

Access Your Priorities

Priorities change with life stages. It is important to have deeply fixed within your consciousness a sense of the ultimate priorities in your life as a central filter which influences all your actions and decisions. But it is also important to review those priorities as they change. What is necessary and demanded at one stage of your life may be inappropriate to the next. The integration of family, children, husband, social being, volunteer, cook, cleaner, worker and achiever continually creates new demands and goals.

Suggestion: Make a list of your current priorities: work, children, husband, social life, diet, exercise, hobbies, education, community. Put them in order—for this month, this year and the next five years. Then examine whether your current behavior reflects those priorities. Are any outmoded or based on old needs? What changes are indicated? Make a second list and write in avenues for action. Have a definite schedule to review and reassess your priorities in the future.

Set Goals and Define Steps to Achieve Them

The first key to success mentioned by former Deputy Attorney General Carol Dinkins was "progressing in a straight line." She knew at an early age that she wanted to become a lawyer. Thus she took the right steps at the right time: college, and then law school. When she married and had children, she did not give up these goals, but simply adjusted her plan.

To accomplish your goals, you must have focus. As the father of one of the authors used to say, if you want to get to San Francisco you could take a train, walk, ride or take a bus, but first you have to know where you were going.

Suggestion: Write down the first of five things that come into your mind following these words:

I want _____

I need _____

To get there, I will _____

Review Your Own Inner-Dialogue, Create Positive Self-Talk

Each person has a real or imaginary "needlepoint pillow" on which is stitched "hokey" and "homey" mottos or slogans. Often little aphorisms guide us through life after we have flung ourselves across the bed, clenched our fists, cursed our mates, taken a three-mile run or hidden our heads under the pillows.

What distinguishes those who persevere against all odds? What self-talk do successful women utilize to help themselves? Clues heard from these women tell us much about their guiding principles and strategies for success.

A friend of Joan Rivers visited her recently and saw this slogan: "Vacations are for amateurs."

One executive remembers the lessons of her role model: "You don't have to find an optimum solution, only a reasonable one."

Other women reported their mottos:

- "I love a road block because it means there is road on the other side."

- "There is no substitute for experience."

- "Keep in the middle of the road."

- "I am willing to give up all other things for a limited period of time."

- "There is a game to it."

- "You can never run away from yourself."

- "Get to work early and always have your shoes shined."

- "Trouble builds character."

- "If I do the best I can in this short life, that's good enough."

- "There is a drive in me that transforms defeat into fuel with which I launch a new offensive."

- "Obstacles and setbacks along the way are nothing more than challenges to test my tenacity and persistence."

- "It must not have been the right thing for me at this time."

- "I think about people whose attitudes I respect most —my grandma and my father. They would never think of themselves as being defeated or set back, nor would they think of my situation in those terms."

- "If everything in one day is going badly, just relax and take one thing at a time. One by one."

- "It's not the end of the world."

- "You can't win them all."

- "There is always an alternative."

- "I learned a lesson."

- "Look on the bright side."

- "You have to learn not to be disappointed with disappointment. You need to accept flaws."

- "I'm not lucky, I'm just damned good."

- "The world does not break down, try one more time, try to be better."

- "If the lift [elevator] to success has stopped, do not stop, try the stairs."

- "Defeat is something I deem very important because it causes me to stop and reevaluate myself and my aspirations."

Suggestion: Review your self-talk. Check your inner dialogue. Make a list of what you say to yourself when you are set back, upset, defeated, puzzled and successful. Does your philosophy help or hinder your mood? Adopt some mottos that inspire a positive attitude.

Look Over the Fence

Among the women interviewed were many who are excellent role models—role models they did not have and which new generations will. The new diversity allows us more and more to draw from the successes and failures of other while broadening our own opportunities.

Since the stereotype prescriptions for successful women's lives are less and less clear, finding models may be more difficult—but not less relevant. There are many women reaching success in different ways.

Look around you. Whose image is appealing to you? Whose image is appalling?

Suggestion: Find three successful women you would like to meet or know more about. Write down necessary steps to find out about them or how to meet them. Determine what works for them.

Understand the Business Environment:
Rules, Language, Behavior, Lifestyle, Trade-Offs

Change can be both rapid and slow. Possibilities seem unlimited and realities are limiting; in this new decade women, in general, seem to be more hopeful and feel freer. However, women find business climates in corporations, newspapers, health professions, etcetera more cautious about change.

You need to learn about the work environment in which you function. What is political and how are the political games played? One woman executive found out in order to win the important appointment she sought, she had to call everyone she knew. She discovered that was the way business was done in her field. That was insider politics.

Explore all options. Don't be afraid to try an unconventional route for getting where you want to go when a more conventional mode of travel won't get you there.

Suggestion: Review your goals. Then list alternative routes for each goal. List necessary actions. Don't evaluate as you are doing this because you may discard potential solutions prematurely. Just brainstorm.

Fantasize and Visualize: Create a World

Create a picture of what you would like to do. Dream about it. Don't think about why it is not possible, just let your mind run free. What would be fun, perfect, stimulating, restful, rewarding? In the best of all possible worlds, what would you like to be doing? Create the whole picture. Who would be with you, what would your office or work space look like? What would your home life be like?

This study found that most successful women fantasized about their careers before attaining their goals. For instance, Debbie Fields says dream and vision were keys to her success. Almost everyone she knew told her she could not succeed in a chocolate-chip cookie business. But she did.

Research has shown that mental rehearsal actually improves physical performance. For example, if a basketball player thinks about the movements involved in approaching the basket and making the shot, his actual game performance improves.

Suggestion: Use your imagination and be creative.

Role play and rehearse new versions of yourself. List three other careers you would like. List five other jobs. Review your present lifestyle in your mind. List alternative lifestyles if yours is unrewarding.

Remember, You Can't Dictate Simpatico.
Go Where You Are Wanted

Suggestion: Spend time thinking about places and people who are receptive to you. Meet the top people in your corporation. Determine whether these are people with whom you could be comfortable. Do you share the values of those people and the organization? Do you share interests? Don't hide your real self but make yourself visible so you can determine early on if you fit into any given situation.

Understand the Differences in Behavioral Style
Between Men and Women

Men and women work differently. It is important to be sensitive to the predominant culture, vocabulary and frames of reference of the people in your chosen field and to find ways of connecting without forsaking your own principles. Be aware of differences in styles and make healthy adaptations. A female internist said that she read the sports page every day so that she would have something to talk about with her male colleagues in the hospital staff rooms. Adapting to other people is not compromise; it is a valuable tool to success.

You need to see differences and to maintain your own distinct qualities. Men may operate one way; women, including yourself, may want to do things differently. Understanding the differences might help you get ahead.

Suggestion: Make a simple list.

I am like my male colleague _____

I am different from them _____

Be Sensitive to Men's Stereotypes about Women

Some men still respond to old sexual role-promptings, and it may be difficult for them to respond professionally if women are sending what they might interpret as sexual signals. The best strategy is not to portray roles that typically elicit a patterned but nonprofessional response.

Articulate Your Career Commitment,
Particularly When You Marry or Become Pregnant

Bosses fear that the demands of family and child-rearing will affect a woman's career. Be sensitive to the common reaction that once a women starts a family, she will no longer be serious about her work. Many employers have had or know of unhappy experiences with new mothers "deserting" their positions. Address this problem by sharing your views about commitment with your superiors.

One woman said that her boss thought she came to work to get away from her children, even though she had told him that she goes home to have a few hours away from work. If you don't tell your boss clearly how you view your job commitments, your behavior will be open to misinterpretation.

Suggestion: Address this problem early by explaining your views. Consider planning children at points in your career when you have established patterns of productivity and commitment.

Gender Defines Us. Let It Be.

Family requirements do not have to hurt your career. They can be dealt with constructively.

Tina Oakland was a nursing mother with a five-month-old daughter and she needed advice. Devotion to her successful advertising career meant delaying a family for years. Now she was a mother with a problem. Tina was scheduled to go to Chicago for five days of important meetings with several male colleagues and clients. She absolutely refused to leave her child. What should she do?

It was suggested by one of our authors, Trudi Ferguson, for whom she came to counseling, that she take the child and a baby-sitter with her to Chicago. She welcomed the idea and departed cheerfully.

A few days later she called from Chicago. She had a growing anxiety about the impression she was making on her clients. She retired immediately after each day's meetings, skipping cocktail hours and dinners. She was often impatient during work sessions because her hungry baby waited in the hotel room. She sensed her clients, all men, felt her distraction.

Tina had revealed that her baby and a sitter were with her, but she was trying to pretend that it did not make a difference. Years in the business world had taught her to keep her personal problems to herself. Mentioning them could be taken as a sign of weakness or as an inability to focus on the important business at hand. Yet now, her male colleagues were growing perplexed and she felt the strain.

She was advised by Trudi to declare the truth about her personal life: I must leave when our business is accomplished. I may not now enjoy the luxury of the social amenities that I value and understand are important. That does not mean I do not value your company or informal exchange or that I always put my family first. I came because this meeting is deeply important to me, but I do have competing pressures. This period in my personal life is tiring and demanding. I hope you will indulge me and view my presence as an indication of my dedication.

Tina delivered the remarks to the men immediately. The responses came as a relief to them and to her. "Well, we had been wondering," said a client. "You always seemed so much in control and so capable, that we never imagined you were being tugged by other things. We interpreted your distraction as a lack of interest and commitment."

The men said her explanation reassured them about her dedication to the project. They were also able to relate to times in their own lives when they were torn by other demands. One man recalled when his youngest son was hospitalized for minor surgery. "It wasn't serious in any way, but it was all I thought about for weeks."

The message is that women should not hide the demands placed on them by their personal situations and life-styles. In fact, explaining them often helps demystify women to male colleagues, many of whom may have had stressful family experiences of their own.

Educate Your Colleagues By Explaining Your Needs and Ambitions

You can educate your colleagues to the meaning of your actions. Even your "desperate outcries" can be explained as functional rather than portentous.

Alternatively, learn to understand more about male responses. Consider the impact of your emotional nature on male colleagues. Make moderate adjustments or offer explanations.

Think about the work styles of the prevailing culture. Figure out how to fit in without changing your basic nature. What are your male colleagues reacting to negatively and what are their stereotypes?

Suggestion: If you feel there is a general lack of understanding between you and your boss or bosses, arrange a lunch or special meeting in which you can discuss overall style.

When you feel there is a specific misunderstanding or irritation, try to address this immediately by explaining your 1) perceptions, 2) explanations, 3) assumptions, 4) motives, 5) needs and 6) meanings.

Unveil the Hidden

Talk about your children. Work out plans for sick child care so you do not have to lie or sneak. Display pictures of your children on your desk. Reveal your complete life so others are aware of your competing demands and can appreciate your commitment to the work environment.

Invite Constructive Criticism

Do not be preoccupied with the belief that anyone who criticizes you does not like you. This could eliminate useful information. Men often are less sensitive to personal criticism and, therefore, get more feedback.

Suggestion: Seek out constructive criticism. Encourage people to give it. Make it easy for people when they try to do so.

Men Can See Women as Moody and Emotional

Many women have been socialized to accommodate and please. You may not be as good at saying "no" or stating your demands up front. Don't let irritation, expectations, or work accumulate to the point where you feel overwhelmed. Express your frustrations clearly and calmly.

Work around Discrimination

Many men respond to stereotypical notions. Discrimination does exist. There is undeniably an "old boys" network, but there are also options for dealing with it.

Suggestion: Ignore it. Joke about it. Go around it. Find receptive men in the environment or leave impossible situations. Educate men to specific discriminatory behaviors that bother you. Often men do not realize that what they are doing is causing a problem. Be ready to state firmly your standards for fair treatment.

Get a Broad Range of Contacts

Get to know the key people in the organization you join. Make or find ways to introduce yourself to a wide range of superiors and subordinates.

Develop Breadth of Experience

Participate in diverse experiences in your business life, such as recruiting boards, social events or professional committees.

Be visible, move into the inner circle of power. Promote yourself. Find ways to connect with people in power. Step out in front and meet key players. Do not be passive, waiting, in the traditional female role, to be approached, rather take the first step. Don't be intimidated by the "good old boys" club. Find other clubs within which to integrate that are not based on gender.

Suggestion: Make a list of the key players, their associates and secretaries. Make a list of activities in which you could participate. Take advantage of a variety of opportunities.

Be Proactive

Invite the important people in your firm to lunch. Drop by their offices. Give them information and reports on your accomplishments. Search for your common experiences. If you have not been invited to the company baseball games or other social gatherings and would like to be, express your interest.

Women not only must recognize their unique abilities, they must also make those abilities visible to their organizations. Do not allow your skills to go unrecognized in the business environment.

Learn Your Shadow Self

Do you have trouble coping with office politics? Is it hard for you to perform certain tasks, recruit clients or be vocal at in-house meetings?

Suggestion: Ask for help in understanding and observing aggressive skills. Find ways to adapt them to your own style. Then test your new skills. Ask for feedback on your progress. Learn to get and use concrete, direct power.

Make Demands

Since most women have been socialized to accommodate and to please, are you less demanding? Have you been trained to be taken care of, not to demand? Have you been raised with the notion that men know what they are doing?

Is money a tough subject? Even powerful newspaper owner Katherine Graham says every time she says the word "money", she has to whisper. Do you still carry taboos about financial demands and compensation?

Suggestion: Ask for what you want. Make sure that your concerns are heard, understood and acted upon. That may involve stating your demands not once but many times.

Keep the Focus

Stand firm on what you want and need. In the early 1970's, before the court-ordered divestiture of AT&T, a consultant was called in to help resolve a problem at company headquarters in Minneapolis. AT&T was considering women for upper-management jobs for the first time. The positions paid well and held the promise of challenging, interesting work. Yet many women were turning down promotions. Company executives were mystified. They genuinely wanted to place more women in higher ranking jobs. They also had federal affirmative action guidelines to meet.

The women approached gave various reasons for passing up promotions; some were personal, some were professional. Each explanation sounded plausible. Yet company executives suspected they were facing a larger problem.

Separate groups of about sixty managers, equally divided between males and females were assembled. The men expressed their frustration. "They just don't want to move," one said. "They're hurting the company." Some men questioned whether women were as capable as men at balancing work and family life. Others questioned their female colleagues' level of commitment and loyalty to the company.

Predictably, the women had different perspectives. It became apparent that women were refusing promotions because of a long-standing company policy that required managers to move from Minneapolis. Briefly, this policy held that managers should gain experience in smaller cities before moving on to more responsible jobs in larger cities. These women were serious about their careers, but they were willing to risk non-advancement because they did not want to move.

The chasm separating the two groups was now obvious. The two factions were brought together, seating the men on one side of the room and the women on the other. Each side was asked to be candid.

A spokesman for the men spoke first. "Why aren't you moving?" he asked. "You are gumming up the works and defying company policy and jeopardizing your own promotions. You need to get experience in the hinterlands to be a good manager and this is the way we have successfully done business at AT&T for years. Why won't you comply?"

"Simple," responded a spokeswomen. "We won't move because we don't want to."

The women had thoroughly assessed their lives and families, their attachment to their community and their children's need for stability. "I probably shouldn't say this," said one, "but from where I sit, career advancement at this company has a price I am not willing to pay."

Other women said they resented the implication that because women were unwilling to move, they were not able to balance personal and profession lives. "The truth is, I think your lives are out of balance," one said pointing to the men. "You sacrifice your families for your careers."

After a few moments another man spoke up. "Frankly, I don't like the policy either, but until this moment, I never dreamed of admitting it." Others quickly agreed.

So a revolution began at AT&T. By verbalizing their dissatisfaction with company policy, women helped crystallize their own feelings as well as those of many of their male counterparts, liberating both genders from years of inner turmoil. The women were more in touch with their needs and were willing to stake their careers on fulfilling these needs. In turn, their beliefs had freed the men to question their own assumptions and corporate demands.

Several years later, during a massive reorganization, AT&T noted with great pride that only three families had to relocate. "Looking back now, as painful as it was at the time, those women helped AT&T prepare for the future," one top executive recently said. "We owe them our thanks."

Suggestion: Women should learn to *follow their instincts and verbalize their needs*, to trust their own methods of evaluation.

Keep the Focus on What You, as a Woman, Want

The women's issues of twenty years ago, flex time, part time job sharing, and child care are now national priorities. Insisting on balance, women make a great contribution to our communal life as well as the work environment.

Learn to Say No

Don't attempt to do and be everything to everyone in your family or work life.

A successful woman in accounting advises, "People are responsive. If I have too much work and say so, they get over it in two days; but if I take more work and I can't do it, they are upset for a long time."

Focus on Necessary Development Work

Separate important and unnecessary work requirements. Do not simply accept the assignments you are given; consider the cumulative impact of those assignments on your career development and on your opportunities for further growth and exposure. Then, once you have paid your dues, lobby for meaningful assignments.

Rehearse and Practice New Roles and Skills

If you are about to enter a new area in which you feel inexperienced and unfamiliar, try some role-playing beforehand. Studies confirm that what has been rehearsed is more automatic and more effective. One company surveyed the population of a small town as to what items they would take out of their houses in case of an emergency. Each resident listed three items. There was, in fact, a fire in that same community a few months later, and the residents took exactly what they had listed in the survey.

Rehearsal gives you an opportunity to hear and understand what you are feeling. Then you have a better chance of detecting flaws or incongruities or inappropriate remarks.

Be Authentic. Relax and Compete

The more authentic you can be, the greater your chances for success become. Don't drain your energy playing a role for which you do not have natural skills. Don't hold back natural behavior for fear of not being taken seriously. Verbalizing complaints may have a competitive advantage. Many husbands chide their wives for excessive emotionalism but at the same time depend on their insight and sensitivity.

Suggestion: Once a month, log in the things that have been effective, fun and successful for you. Then answer the following two questions each month:

1. I like myself best at work when I _____
2. Success to me is _____

Keep this log for a year and review it to see central themes of your *authentic* self and your evolving definition of success.

Get Support

An important lesson is there is strength in numbers. Find people who have similar values and beliefs. Support each other in the areas where you share commonalities and problems. You should have support in both your professional and personal life.

Suggestion: Find two or more people in your life and develop relationships of trust. Do not count on one person as your sole support in too many categories. He or she may be overburdened. It is difficult and limiting for one person to be your support in every area of your life.

Making Periodic Assessments of Your Goals and Priorities

Build assessment points into your life and work that will allow you to monitor your satisfaction and progress.

Be optimistic that there are alternative routes. Develop and use a philosophy that will provide inspiration as well as sustain you in moments of defeat. The chart which follows can help you evaluate your personal support systems.

SUPPORT SYSTEM

Needs of *Support for*		Fill in names of people who support you in your *professional/personal life*
Isolation	People who like me. People who include me and make me feel welcome.	_____ _____ _____
Self-image	People who confront me and make me feel good.	_____ _____

Marginability	People who are like me and share the same values attitudes and perspectives	_____
		_____
		_____

Agreement/ approval	People who make me feel I'm on the right track.	_____
		_____
		_____

Competency	People who affirm my competence	_____
		_____
		_____

Measurance	People who give me a chance to be listened to with sympathy and interest	_____
		_____
		_____

Crisis overload	People who can be counted on to help me in crisis overload	_____
		_____
		_____

| Imposing limits | People who help me when I get ideas that are excessive and off the beam. People who help me correct distortions. | _____ |
| | | _____ |

Material rewards	People who give me wonderful things	_____
		_____
		_____

Dig in and Push Forward

Accept anxiety and temporary discomfort. These interviews revealed many stories of women who endured periods of anxiety. New behavior and change brings tense moments. Do not wait until worry or anxiety fades to move your life forward.

One young woman spoke of complaining. She didn't know if she would be able to give a presentation since she didn't feel well. Her supervisor counseled, "Most of the work of the world is done by people who don't feel well."

Suggestion: Figure out a plan to deal with your anxiety. Breathing exercises, self-talk, physical exercise, reading about coping with stress, and keeping track of those times that, despite the anxiety, you acted and succeeded.

Be Forgiving

Good judgement is learned through bad judgement. All the women in this survey spoke about the difficulties they faced trying to create new roles. According to each, the road is sometimes very bumpy. Assume that problems arise from noble attempts at new definitions. Take care of yourself and give yourself the benefit of the doubt. Remember these successful women tried, failed, cried, fell, got up, persevered and eventually succeeded.

Suggestion: List your three most recent failures. Reframe them and decide what you learned from them and how you can utilize what you have learned in the future.

CHAPTER THIRTEEN

HOW-TO FOR CORPORATIONS

"Businesses have to realize that families are going to continue; they are just the law of the land."
Disgruntled Accountant

The integration of women into the workforce is not complete; the integration of married women who have children into the workforce has only begun. Total assimilation may still take generations.

But the reflections of the women in this study—along with our conclusions—allow the suggestions of a broad-based program for corporations that will increase their sensitivity to the issues, tie women's issues to the bottom line, meet women's needs, effectively utilize women's unique talents, and promote clearer understanding of women's behavior in the corporate setting.

Corporate awareness is the common thread most needed, according to these women. They feel the final solutions lie in institutions recognizing and adjusting to the fact that women with children are important in the work force. Institutions must find ways to fit them into the corporate structure and utilize their talents while satisfying corporate needs of loyalty and productivity.

Sensitivity

Over and over again women refer to the need for general sensitivity to the issues that control women's life. There are competing demands and pulls of marriage, pregnancy, nursing, birthing, childrearing, care-taking and striving for accomplishment and contribution. If women experience a lack of sensitivity from a key individual in an organization, then that lack of sensitivity can be projected onto the organization as a whole. Sensitivity means corporate awareness that children are a legitimate hope and concern. It means women do not have to lie in order to take time off to attend a sick child. It may mean not scheduling meetings at 7 a.m. when there is no child care. It may mean that corporations are proactive in our society to assist the reformulation of other institutions to accommodate the reality of corporate life.

Social institutions such as schools and recreational organizations are aimed at women who stay home and raise children. But both schools and corporations must help the adjustment to the changing reality—supported by statistics—that a majority of married women with children work. Therefore, school hours of 9 a.m. to noon or 3 p.m., recreation requiring driving and attendance during the work day, and a nine-to-five employment situation may present major difficulties to working women.

HOW TO:

1. Increase sensitivity to women.

This can be done through education, discussion, observation, data gathering and commitment. Corporations need to review the subtle attitudes that infuse a variety of business positions and reactions to women. For example, have we separated the concept of management from maleness? Managers have to be tough, political, independent, expert, competitive and secretive. But we know there are many women managers who are very effective and who have very different qualities.

Attitudes that need to be reviewed: (a) Reflecting negative views about the possibility of women combining career and family, e.g. the "Mommy Track", (b) Inputing a lack of seriousness to women's careers, (c) Making or listening to remarks about the importance of women staying at home to raise children, (d) Assumptions that clients will have difficulty relating to women professionals, (e) Lack of sensitivity to women as a natural part of the professional population, (f) Stereotypes about women's lack of aggressiveness and toughness, (g) Off-color jokes and crude remarks about women, (h) Harsh inflexible attitudes about the necessity of long hours as a *sine qua non* of hard work and (i) Attitudes that women are too emotional.

2. **Search out and review subtle negative attitudes that reflect on women's ability to combine the multiple roles successfully.**

Every women in this study identified the need for further progress in the area of child care assistance and sensitivity. Even the women who worked in the most accommodating organizations had problems. Suggested solutions ranged from on-site or close to work day-care to relief of mental anxiety by child care referrals or financial credits. The basic feeling was that child care is not just a women's issue but that it is a family issue. Its successful solutions are related to the general social welfare not just of individual mothers but of total families.

The women interviewed for this study are the lucky ones, since they have reached top positions in their careers. In most cases, they love their jobs and, therefore, feel less conflicted about the reduced hours with their children. This lack of conflict correlates to better adjustment in their children. These women also realize that they are able to afford better in-home or private child care than most women who work.

Being top moneymakers, they have the financial resources to relieve many of the maintenance burdens of life, such as cooking and cleaning, so that what time they do have can maximally be spent with their children. As Dianne Arnold stated, "Most women have to work, often at jobs they don't like. And even then they have to scramble to piece it together in unconventional ways. There are fewer systems for accreditation or training of in-home child care givers. There is little public recognition for the unorthodox mixture that is thrust upon these women in order to help their families survive financially. Women in typical jobs have neither the education or the support to assist them. Their struggle is our communal loss as it impacts the successful rearing of THEIR children and OUR citizens."

An article in the *Atlantic Monthly*, reflecting on the differences between American and Japanese societies, focused attention on the role of women. It acknowledges that unfortunate constraints that have historically been placed on Japanese women continue to limit their full participation in public life. But it also reminded us of the social benefit of such sexual restraint. Those women are raising and educating their children and that is a public good. This suggests that Americans learn something about the real requirements of proper child rearing in terms of commitment, time, energy, attention, partnership and the real social consequences for a healthy, productive society.

A serendipitous, last minute, rushed, haphazard program at best does not serve our families, our work force, our institutions or our society as a whole. This is an issue for important public discussion with businesses and corporations taking the lead. It is a business issue. It is a corporate issue. It is a societal issue.

3. Commit to study and innovation about child care assistance.

Establish a *task force* consisting of mothers, fathers, school administrators and business management to explore feasible options. Consider the possibility of *sick leave:* granting a finite number of days available for the use of parents themselves or for their children. *Personal days* can be provided to all employees so that parents have the necessary flexibility to attend important school functions or deal with other school matters. *Child care centers* could be set up on-site by employers. As an alternative, employers could invest financial support for existing centers operated by others or even consider establishing joint ventures with other employers to establish joint centers. *Special on-the-job child care days* could be considered when school is canceled due to inclement weather or to introduce the child to work atmospheres. *Child care referrals* can be handled with a certified list of credible child care professionals in the local community to be used by employees. Employers might also solicit interest from retiring employees or friends and relatives of existing employees. Employers might also consider employing and training a cadre of available child care people employed by the company itself to be used in urgent business emergencies. *Child care travel policies* can be set. Parents who must travel for business purposes can be reimbursed for child care expenses incurred solely because of their business trip. *After school programs* might be considered to help fill the gap between school dismissal and quitting time. *Busing:* employees could be encouraged to bring their children to the work site and then have those children bussed to special camps or programs.

Many of the problems married women with children encounter start with initial interviews. Outdated male prejudices against working mothers may dominate company hiring practices. A realistic discussion in top management needs to take place in which feminine maturity and business skills are taken into consideration as well as their commitment to professional and corporate life. More women who are mothers should be involved in the hiring process so that potential female employees will have greater comfort in the discussions and get a truer picture of life for women in that organization.

Nancy Evans, former president and publisher of Doubleday, contributes these suggestions for corporations to consider: "Corporations can simply have space where kids can be brought in, not as day care, but where kids can come in a few times, for the mom or dad."

She also suggests that the lines between workplace and family life should not be so blurred; children should not be kept so separate. She sees the fastest growing organizations to be on the West Coast, many run by Baby Boomers and men who want to be with their kids, too. Old line organizations are the slowest to adapt new thinking.

"And women have to get out of the closet. The popular media does a disservice in writing about working women." Evans goes on, "We have to get to the nitty gritty of what women's lives are really like. There is a body of wisdom, and it's all those little things that make a difference."

4. Oppose the "Mommy Track"

Through this study we found women not only can but do combine successful family life with top careers. Women do not have, nor should they have, to make a choice. Corporations are equally responsible not just to accommodate women, but to help them devise ways in which they can enter and work without reducing them to the status of junior executive or responsible assistant. Corporations should not be afraid to hire women with children because having children does not mean having to settle for a second-class career. There is no overriding reason why women with children who wish to cannot handle mother roles and employment and still participate in top management just as men do.

Almost all the women in this study expressed opposition to the notion of a "Mommy Track." They recognized that the jobs they now hold could not be done on a part time basis. Moreover, they are aware that if they want the power and authority that goes along with their jobs, they must commit. However, they resist the notion that such committment means they must give up family lives.

Corporations can resist the "Mommy Track" by actively promoting women within the ranks and by recognizing that those women can rise to the top while choosing to enjoy marriage and families just as their male counterparts do.

5. Be open and sensitive to differing styles.
Look for results, success.

Do not be limited by one image of success and effectiveness. There are different modes of productivity and impact. Help women *educate male colleagues as to how women work* by explaining needs and making sure desperate outcries are viewed as functional rather than portentous. Women can learn to understand the impact of their emotional nature on male colleagues. Invite and use constructive criticism. Help women get feedback despite the male stereotype that women will react too emotionally and that women may take criticism too personally. Be sensitive to stereotypical sexual clues: women work differently from men, and women work differently from one another.

One newspaper executive admitted that she had mixed feelings when a Harvard graduate and top performer had a child in her mid-thirties and then decided she wanted to stay home with her child. "That's just what corporations expect, and it gives all women a bad name," she said. But one woman's choice is not that of all women.

In the process of doing research for this study, we found ourselves sometimes generalizing unfairly. One would identify a problem or potential problems and try to find confirmation from the next respondent—only to discover it was an isolated opinion. A top female lawyer lamented how persuasive was the impact of toughness on her personality and how that interfered with her nurturing side. But this was not true of the next woman. For her it was an obvious self-limitation she put on herself.

A newspaper executive could not even relate to the idea of self-limits. "The issue for women in the nineties is real power, the excitement and the meat." In contrast, a lawyer said, "I have no ambition beyond this position. Power doesn't excite me."

The many perceived differences, between men and women and women and women, are sometims semantics and emphasis. But youthful beliefs that everyone is really the same are, in reality, not true either. People are fundamentally different and, increasingly, corporations need to recognize and respect that.

6. **Solicit input from women individually. Avoid stereotypical assumptions about all women. Create opportunities for women to express themselves and hear what they say.**

Corporations need to pay attention to the subtle assumptions that are implied in company rules. What are the unwritten norms, practices, assumptions about men and women and management and effectiveness? What are the assumptions about female deficiencies and strengths versus creative looks at problem solving.

7. **Systematically examine unstated assumptions governing performance, desirability, inviolates of management, women's preferences.**

Create a position of ombudsman or an informal designate whose job is to monitor informal prejudice within the organization. What is working and what is not working? Where are men and women getting stuck? Where is the tension, discomfort or lack of understanding? What are women saying? Where and why are they leaving? Where and why are they well-received and productive? Have this individual report at specific intervals about women's status and needs in the organization.

Help men and women sort out their reactions to modern lifestyles and difficult roles. One of the most damaging assumptions is that women or men should be able to figure it all out by themselves.

8. Create counseling sessions, provide college courses to explore and train women and men for more effective family and work life and how to integrate the two.

Make use of support groups and encourage participation by both men and women.

9. Make top women visible in the organization. Promote qualified women to positions of real power.

Have visible role models. Women who are powerful in the organization have to be vocal, disclose their stories, speak up for other women's and family needs. Younger women need to know what top women "look like" so that they feel enabled. Women need to define part of the corporate culture.

10. Establish gender task forces to administer mechanics of new programs.

Each organization is different. Demographics and needs differ. There is a need for systematic review of policies impacting women. A task force can initiate and monitor the specifics of programs that would be appropriate for a particular corporation.

Suggestions:

Sponsor gender workshops—discuss women's issues, discuss men's issues, discuss gender issues. Educate managers about the changing workforce in this workshop and make it available to all senior executives and to their key subordinates.

Publish a reading list of important discussion on women's perspectives, sexual interactions in the workplace, child care options and the like.

Establish and publish a maternity policy.

Create child care assistance— this could range from on-site employer-sponsored day care to a child care reference list.

Create an on-going data gathering system that collects statistical data in such areas as: how many women leave the organization, at what points in their careers, the numbers of women in comparable positions and what they are paid as compared to men, reasons for their leaving, demographics, such as the number of women with children, as well as attitudinal data about their feelings of value, power treatment and contentment.

Provide career counseling for women.

Provide access by women to top levels in the organizations and offer special feedback sessions for two way communication.

Increase informal contacts with scheduled lunches, sports tickets distributed to women, social events that are family oriented.

Build sensitivity to gender issues into performance evaluation.

11. Offer spousal relocation assistance programs.

Women may be more willing to relocate with the company if the family economic unit is not disadvantaged. TRW has been a leader in this field and has spent considerable sums to help place the spouses of their top women employees who are required to move. Additionally, they also offer counseling assistance to women's partners.

Resource: Careers found that the form of spousal assistance ranked most helpful by women executives was the placement of spouses through informal contacts with other companies. Job counseling ranked second.

When Mobil Corporation moved its headquarters from New York City to suburban Washington, seventy-five percent of their workers were in dual-career marriages. That meant that Mobil had to also find jobs for teachers, nurses, sale representatives, entrepreneurs, editors and other folk who weren't part of its employee base. That amounted to over seven hundred people.

Mobil employed the talents of Resource Careers, who helped counsel and place those spouses. In addition, they administered a questionnaire designed to determine their needs, gave a seminar on preparing for job searches and drafting resumes, and established an information center with Mobil, determining employers with projected needs for employees in the new area. They also created a loose consortium of companies interested in hiring executive spouses. The spouses received individual counseling on job hunting and there was even a support group where spouses could meet and share advice.

12. Tie Costs To Bottom Line
Information should be used to show the costs in recruiting, retention, and loss of talent to corporate profits and to social and family health in general.

13. Publish Options
A stated policy related to maternity time, and promotion of women spells out options for aspiring women. Women need to see what can be in store for them rather than guess or depend on their own ability—at a vulnerable time—to negotiate reasonable alternatives.

THINGS CORPORATIONS MUST *NOT* DO INCLUDE:

1. Let the old male chauvinist pig attitudes rule. The out of date must not be allowed to set the tone of corporate hiring and promotion policies.
2. Ignore. It is not possible to ignore these issues. They impact women individually and they impact corporations collectively.
3. Let discomfort rule. We all need help. We cannot allow discomfort to prevail. We must meet and confer and get these problems out in the open. PROBLEM SEEING IS PROBLEM SOLVING.
4. Keep your distance. Sometimes when a person or problem is uncomfortable, we want to keep our distance. But the solution to these problems, and often

to management difficulties, is anti-instinctual. In other words, our instinct is to move away from the problems and avoid people we don't like or understand. But we must go against our instincts to escape and discuss the problem.

5. We must not separate women and family and work. This has happened for too long and to too many women at a great cost. It is unreal and untrue and has dire consequences if corporations continue this myth.

6. Don't assume the needs of professional women are all the same.

7. Don't assume this issue is solved. This is a subtle problem that impacts society and can create individual fears, anxiety and doubts.

New Management Styles

During the 70's concerns were focused on legal issues for women and in the 80's women's access to business was the thrust. The push of the 90's is away from sameness and equality of opportunity toward a new synthesis of management styles.

Material on new options for corporations about ways to work can be obtained from such associations as The Women's Bureau, Women's Employment Institute, Catalyst and Resource Careers. These offer material, resources, training and bibliographies to assist corporations in training and developing change. There are also consultants in organization development who work exclusively with women's issues in corporations. The Committee of Two Hundred is a gathering place for highly successful women in this country. Corporations should avail themselves of all these options to make or support appropriate changes.

CHAPTER FOURTEEN

TIPS AND TACTICS FOR "MOMMIES" IN THE BOARDROOM

"I have always tried to blur the lines between work and my personal life—and keep them blurred. The notion of balancing is outmoded; blending is what is important."

Nancy Evans
—Former Publisher of Doubleday

None of the women in this survey claim to have found all the right answers to handling the roles of mother and career woman, but interestingly all the women would choose both roles again. Despite the difficulties encountered they feel that the satisfactions are well worth it.

During the interviews, each one was asked for "tips" on what strategies they used as well as the thoughts and attitudes which enabled them to fulfill their many responsibilities.

Following are important highlights from these interviews.

Actions

Work close to home. Dentist Nancy Schort felt this was a central strategy for her success. She lives within walking distance of her office and does in fact walk, combining time for exercise and getting to work. It has also allowed her the psychological comfort of knowing that her children are close to handle emergencies. When her baby-sitter called to report that Nancy's daughter had broken her arm, Nancy was able to say "bring her right over to the office." It turned out that the arm was only sprained, but the point was that Nancy could respond to the crisis without great havoc.

Choose the father of your children carefully. There is no point if you have to fight a constant battle with your husband over your intentions to have a successful career path. You have to be sure he is going to he supportive.

Run your business to prevent or limit interoffice stress. Doctor Amy Roseman felt that a major stress of competitive doctoring was linked to monetary partnership draws based on patients seen and specific work done. Her office was able to pinpoint that stress and switch to a different criteria—equal financial returns to the five partners. Amy says realistically that this system works for them because "I work with non-lazy people." They have instituted paid maternity leave, but the one male partner can have paid educational leave. Also, they each take a six-week sabbatical every five years. This system increases the diversity in their total practice and promotes each one's career with support, understanding and time off. Plus they can help one another develop and train in their individual specialties.

Don't get on a treadmill; take on realistic financial obligations. Roseman offered other suggestions to limit the financial obligations so that it does not become yet another driving pressure. Her own example was choosing to buy a house in the volatile Los Angeles real estate market that was comfortable rather than luxurious.

Reduce expectations for output (and pay) while pregnant. This formula worked for one lawyer who is highly respected and powerful in her law specialty. But she was deliberate about not expecting to get the same financial draw from her law firm when she was pregnant and nursing. Since she did not expect the same renumeration during this time, she was not overstressed or resentful when her cut was less. She accepted the fact that while her skills and competencies were at least co-equal, her time and inclination for that period were not.

Get good child care; you can't leave home without it. A tip from most of the women was to find the best child care you can afford whether it is household help, babysitters, childcare facilities, or schools with before and after hours care. Have back-up support systems in place in case of illness or accidents. This might be family help or friends with whom you can develop a partnership relationship. You and your husband should develop a priority system in which one of you can be available during a critical period.

Establish rituals. Family customs such as Saturday outings, holiday celebrations and special trips that children can count on enhance the working family's relationship. Formulating dependable times to be together communicates affection, and needs and goals become even more important when quality time is short. Every Christmas vacation, Barbara Boxer takes her family to Kona Village, Hawaii, where they can relax and luxuriate in each other's company. Another executive contributed her formula, "I don't do dinners. All my business is finished at the end of the business day. My children are preteens, so dinner can be late. But even when they were small, they'd have a snack and we'd all eat together and talk over our days."

Pick a field in which you have some control over your life. Astronaut Anna Fisher recognizes she was once naive and thought you could do it all. "At one time I thought you always get good childcare. That was it. Period," she says. Now she advises giving much thought to a career you can scale down, leave or control for a period of years.

Install a computer terminal at home with a modem. Jennifer Lawson was able to do most mommy tasks like putting dinner on the table, putting her son to bed, be a physical presence in the house, and still do work after he went to bed through the advent of modern technology.

Take a personal vacation every other year. Even if it is just an overnighter, Lawson finds respite and renewal by taking a vacation alone every other year. During this short time off she thinks about her life and goals. What does she want in the future? How can she change her life and her family's life to give them all more satisfaction?

If you shift gears, put people on notice. Women may take time out physically or emotionally during childrearing. But there is no reason why they can't re-enter. However, it can be confusing to colleagues. Dianne Arnold suggests we put others on the alert and explain our intentions.

Have a support system. What could be better and of more help than a mother living in the same town. Marcy Tiffany specifically moved to the house she chose because it was near two grandmothers. But if this is impossible, a supportive working mothers group or networking is important.

Cluster your work. Congresswoman Barbara Boxer sometimes works straight through the week including Saturday mornings if necessary, but then allots a chunk of free time for family. She mentions that she would hate to do what some of her colleagues do—which is to work on both days of the weekend—so that one never has family time.

Pick doable projects. The goals most of these women work for are enormous. Their combined advice is that you must pick and choose the tasks that can be accomplished one by one when your worktime is limited by family constraints.

Be organized. When one executive is at home, she prioritizes tasks, then groups them together—such as clothes shopping in one-day-whirlwinds twice a year, catalog or telephone shopping in between. Another executive offered this suggestion: find companies that offer food plans; you can buy meat and staples on a three-months basis and fill in with lighter food shopping once a week.

Those are some of the actions successful women with children use to continue and implement their work lives while fulfilling family responsibilities. Just as important, according to them, are positive attitudes toward balancing their roles.

Believe in the long run. This seemed to be a strongly held outlook voiced by the majority of the women in this study. Merrie Spaeth said you usually get another chance to do things. If you are not happy you can either restructure your job or get a new one. Your family remains persistent not just in career terms, but on day-to-day terms. Amy Roseman offered, "Always look at the big picture. There is nothing so important today that can't be put off. Pace yourself. Balance. You can't do everything at the same time."

Marjorie Fine used the same words about seeing the big picture and Carol Dinkins contributed, "Look beyond the discomforts and inconveniences of day-to-day life and focus on what you want to gain."

Sharon Flaherty added, "Have a long term perspective. Sometimes I think what I've accomplished in the last thirty days isn't much, but if I look at the last nine months, there is real movement and it gives me the energy to keep going. From day-to-day all I can see is a huge stack of paper on my desk."

Sort out priorities. Realize that you have limited time and dual responsibilities. Give up activities—at least for a limited time—that complicate your life. Work and family are the only two priorities for many of these women. "My only cultural event is *Sesame Street,*" stated corporate executive Pam Flaherty.

Reduce guilt. In combining dual roles, try to accent positive attitudes. Most women experience some guilt associated with being a working parent. But for most it is not debilitating. As one film producer stated, "It is kind of like a weight problem, just something I have to live with."

Again and again women said they would not be very good mothers if they were at home full time. Marcy Carsey felt she would be hovering and over involved, probably running to school every two minutes, interfering and being detrimental to her children.

Carol Dinkins described a grumpy day off. After being at home all day, her daughter looked at her and said, "You wouldn't want to do this all the time." Carol agreed. "I kept coming back to the fact that if I stayed home all the time, I would be difficult and unpleasant to deal with."

Helen Blumin sees herself as intense and would not want to focus all her intensity on a child. She feels this might happen if she were to spend all her time at home.

Elizabeth Blalock illustrates the attitudinal ability of making the best of what you have. She has been a divorced single parent since the time she was seven months pregnant with her son. "The kids turned out wonderfully. They're nice and well behaved. It's helpful for kids to have a clear sense of what is expected and when. Sometimes it's easier when they only have one source telling them these things." Her most important tactic, she says, was to have a positive attitude toward her children.

Make choices and don't second guess yourself. "Early on you have to make the basic decision to work hard and if you haven't decided that, it is constant turmoil. I was convinced my kids would survive if I did." This is what Sandra Day O'Connor said about the time her son hurt his head and had to be taken to the hospital by a neighbor. "I always did the best I could and never once looked back and agonized."

Dianne Arnold related that when people ask what sacrifices she has made, she says, "I prefer to think of them as choices not sacrifices."

One woman says she never complains to her own daughters about the traveling she does. Since she doesn't feel unhappy about it, she thinks the same feeling is communicated to her daughters and they don't complain.

Many women said if you're not happy with your life, the children can not be happy. And even in their own minds, all these ambitious, active, directive women felt they would not be happy being at home full time.

Set realistic goals while aiming high. It is important to recognize that change is slow and that the acceptance of women's rights to have families and work at top levels actually happens on an individual basis. It is important to have dreams but to be realistic in setting more immediate goals.

Other less philosophic and more basic practical advice surfaced in the shape of suggested nonperfectionist attitudes:

If a pot is greasy, I don't care. You have to let go of appearances. Women described not cooking, cleaning or doing routine tasks, or accepting the myriad of social invitations in order to adequately handle more important aspects of parenting and job performance.

It doesn't have to be perfect. One executive offered this model tip, the recognition of which is comforting and definitely a good change. "By admitting it isn't perfect, we can commiserate with each other and get on with accomplishing what we can both at home and at work." The worst scam ever put on a woman is perfectionism; perfect wife, unfailing mother and flawless executive. This concept only sets women up to agonize, thinking if they could only work harder, that fantasy may all come true when in truth it is an impossible dream.

Things go wrong. You have to be able to change your schedule to deal with your children when problems arise even if it is inconvenient. Crises occur at the office and you may have to cope with them at times which inconvenience your family.

Enjoy your children. The years go by fast and it is easy to lose sight of this fact. Don't let yourself get bogged down by mundane tasks. Take time to make time with your children.

Recognize that you won't always be going at this clip. Children grow up. You won't always have to split your time between home life and career.

Develop selective memory loss.

Buy stockings in bulk. This is a tip from Nancy Evans, who has suffered many times from running late, going to her stocking drawer, only to find none or stockings with runs.

"If you go into an organization and all you see is women typing and men in the offices, forget it!" is the advice of Cathleen Black of *USA Today.*

Use the same Christmas decorations.

Get television trays for the inevitable dinners in bed.

Get rid of math anxiety. Don't be encumbered by the old quantative anxieties women felt.

One woman who has made her mommy/executive role work is Cathleen Black, forty-six, publisher of *USA Today*. She answers the question of how does one juggle the roles of top executive and mother of a three-year old by saying, "some days are better than others. It helps that we have a fabulous American nanny. She is the reason this works. I also have an extremely supportive husband, a lawyer, and we take it day by day."

Her son is adopted. He is an easy baby and has been from the start. According to her, the company has been as supportive as they can be. She recently attended a newspaper convention in Los Angeles and took her child and nanny with her. "But I try to keep my family and work separate. I didn't stay in the same hotel where the convention was held and I didn't drag my baby to the meetings. On the other hand, I think the people I work with like the fact I have a baby. It humanizes me. But I try to be smart about the two. The baby is part of my life, but he is not the only part."

Cathleen's husband reminds her it is better not to get too worked up about the conflicts. She has a friend who is a doctor whom she describes as very conflicted. "I honestly don't feel that way," she adds.

I spoke to her on a Friday. She had taken the red eye from the coast the previous night so she could be at home in the morning, go to work during the day, and attend the weekly children's play group late Friday afternoon. Although she does not attend the play group on a weekly basis, she likes to occasionally attend to see the other mothers and how the kids are growing.

Her nanny starts the day at 7:45 a.m. and works until about 6:30 p.m., the time when Cathleen gets home. When hiring her nanny, Cathleen made it very clear to her that her hours had to be very flexible. "She had to enjoy travel and also be willing to work one or two nights a week if I was out of town or we were going out in Washington." She didn't want a nanny coming in and leaving two weeks later because it hadn't been understood that some days would be longer than others. "Now I don't feel a lot of stress if I don't walk in the door at 6:30 p.m. Most women have to watch the clock so they can get home and pick up kids at child care. I couldn't do that. It would add a level of anxiety with which I could not deal."

The other thing she says helps is not telling yourself that you are the best mother in traditional ways, because you're not. One problem Cathleen has had is a kind of "power trip" with her baby's nanny when they are all together at a social function. "There are hidden conflicts, judging from my past, and the question of 'Who's in charge?' But I realize that is natural for both of us, and we are able to talk about it." she says. But Cathleen does agree upon the kind of care the nanny gives the baby; she is devoted and creative and gives lots of love and affection, doing what Cathleen would want, "Plus, our nanny is incredibly responsible. She is simply a terrific young woman.

"I know I'm not the perfect mother," Cathleen continues, "some days are harder than others, especially if I have to be away. Still, I really have an intimate relationship with my child and he seems to be very responsive and outgoing. My husband is also outgoing and enjoys being with him. So the baby gets a lot of love from three people. Plus, my husband's parents live near us, so we have the wonderful benefit of grandparents, too."

Cathleen was married at twenty-five and divorced at thirty. She didn't remarry until she was thirty-eight. "I always felt I wanted to have children, but I knew it wasn't going to be this all consuming thing. My husband was less interested, which was odd because he is the oldest of five children. Maybe he felt he already had done some of his parenting."

Cathleen comes from a traditional family in which her father was a successful small businessman. She was very close to him. He died when she was twenty-three. Her mother was a traditional housewife and was more conflicted about Cathleen's career. She worried that Cathleen would be a single, career woman without a family of her own.

"I never had any problem with adoption," she says when thinking back. "My husband was more hesitant. I was very serious about adopting and felt if it risked the marriage, it risked the marriage."

Later, she realized part of his resistance had been voiced in a comment to her: "Cathie, I don't even have that much of your time."

In reference to having more children, I asked if they would have more. "One is doable," she said, "and we would be delighted if another dropped into our laps, but I don't think that's going to happen."

Cathleen was asked what she thought organizations might do to support women who want to have children. She replied, "As an employer, you want to be responsive and enlightened. We need more innovation regarding part-time and flex-time. There will be conflicts and problems, too. When I learned that one of our senior sales representatives was told by her doctor she had to stay in bed with her pregnancy for three months, I assure you, I didn't feel much like a feminist. It put a strain on the office and definitely affected sales negatively. But we got through it. People in responsible positions have to realize that business goes on. On the plus side, in one corporate headquarters, we have a children's day care facility located across the street. Women in our company are thrilled. In my opinion if women have fulfilling jobs and enlightened managers, they want to come back. If they have lousy jobs, they don't rush back—unless they absolutely have to."

She offered these additional tips:

"Women now have options. They can really choose what they want and how much they want. Five years ago, if you didn't make partner, you simply would kill yourself. Now there is enough diversity to decide. If you treat women well some will return to work early and some won't, but it allows a woman a chance to define what she wants and a chance to change that definition over time.

"Today women are looking for new challenges. However, the majority of power is still held by men and it won't be given up easily. But more and more corporations are realizing the tremendous benefits that women bring them and are beginning to offer the opportunities in growing numbers. I am hopeful that the workplace will become a more hospitable environment for women with families."

The last outstanding characteristic the women in this survey have in common—and one which is significant for those who have chosen the dual roles of parent and executive—is that they are good managers of their own dilemmas. When one must balance the roles of mother and working woman, nothing is in a steady state. These women have accepted the fact that their lives evolve daily. They live with family and career predicaments and work at fulfilling their desires and responsibilities without spinning out of control. The sense of struggle is ever present but these women try to manage their lives effectively and to find satisfaction.

It is just this sometimes graceful, sometimes precarious management of the ever present challenge that sets these women—married and successful with children—apart. These women, despite upsets, faithfully handle the daily living process and the problem solving. Successful advertising executive Adrienne Hall has expressed this stressful, but exalting, experience by choosing the image of successful women balancing on a tightrope, forever moving precariously forward but with elegant excitement.

"By its very nature, balance implies being able to keep your toes on the tightrope, to make it across the years with enough resilience to swing a little, love a little, laugh a little. And it means that, even hanging by a thread, you never fall off."

WHAT DO WOMEN OF THE '90S WANT?

"There is a drive in me that transforms defeat into fuel with which I launch a new offensive."
—Successful Woman Executive and Mother

The original objective of this inquiry was to help understand whether married women with children can and have stayed on the main track to reach top level career destinations and, at the same time, remain caring, involved parents—or whether such women should be placed on alternate tracks in order to fulfill their obligations as wives and mothers while working.

On reviewing the statistics and portraits produced by this study we conclude simply that if mothers want to work in executive capacities it *can be done* with support, confidence and energy. This is not to say that, at present, such success is being achieved by women in great numbers. Such a statement was neither our thesis nor our rationale.

Nor have we sought to point out the discriminatory and glass ceiling factors which preclude some women from entering top management. Instead, we have focused on women who succeeded, pointing out that such theories as the "Mommy Track" are debilitating myths. This study shows there are high achievers who are also caring mothers.

None of the women who were interviewed expressed the sense that their jobs, albeit in glamourous or stimulating industries, outweighed caring about, or for, their children. However, it is also clear that few envisioned work versus family as either/or choices, but rather as parts of their composite lives. All agreed there are many difficult —and some unnecessary—struggles to find a balance in combining those dual roles in our existing society.

Our hope is that the disclosures of the problems and successes of these women and these corporations will stimulate further searches for permanent solutions to integrating women who desire families and have high level career goals.

In reviewing these disclosures, seven main conclusions about the women we studied become apparent:

1. They have created new scripts. There is no one pattern for success. The women in this book seemed free of conventional ideology about achievement or femininity, raising children, kinds of good marriages or what success looks like and how to get there. They have rejected the restraints of conventional scripts, choosing to create, instead, new storylines.

2. They have improvised new life patterns. The picture of the normal patterns for families usually depicted did not exist in most instances. Instead, we found unusual new life styles—bold, creative, ad hoc, and matter of fact— invented to accommodate these successful working mothers in 1990 America.

3. They had diverse backgrounds. There were heritages of many different kinds: Mayflower society and immigrants, privileged and poor, uneducated and graduate educations, raised in single parent homes and raised in conventional families. All their careers involved demands, and rejections, and pioneering negotiations for status, individual accommodations and extraordinary sacrifices and efforts.

4. They adopted guilt-reducing strategies. Strikingly, these women all had gritty attitudes that lessened what, for most, at times, seemed inescapable guilt. Their perceptions were that you just have to be a "good enough" mother; that as full time mothers they would be too intense and overly involved; that they had to satisfy and fulfill themselves; that a happy mother makes a happy child. Their attempts at guilt reduction seemed to go hand in hand with their sense of confidence. Their strategies illuminate ways to help other women and society lessen the guilt and tensions of dual roles and create new options for women.

5. They accepted the struggle. There was no straight line. All these women had struggles and detours, tensions between work and family, problems commuting, being fired and laid off; at different periods in their careers they were ignored, bypassed, and defeated. The tensions seemed particularly great for women with younger children. Yet the one quality shared by all was the ability to endure and move on to achievement.

6. They found support. None of these women achieved success alone. They enlisted the help of amazing partners; some were house-husbands, car pool drivers, cooking mates, primary nurturer fathers, grandparents, therapists, child care providers, school systems, and organizations that provided child care in one form or another. In each case, the successful woman found and made the needed connection in order to function effectively as both mother and achiever.

7. They made lifelong adjustments and readjustments. Women went into therapy, remarried, went back to school, created new types of work situations and changed locations and professions. Combining dual roles is seemingly impossible without the ability to accept temporary solutions while searching for permanent ones.

FUTURE QUESTS

The results of our study show that, more than anything, women want a superior quality of life in all areas. They want the ability to contribute at the highest professional levels and they want the opportunity to participate at the highest level in their family lives. They want to maximize the use of their professional and creative talents and to minimize psychological distress. They want symmetry between career and family.

The women represented here indicated the need for expanded opportunities for contribution: volunteerism, self-development and family activities. While working at the top of their professions, they want freedom from the excessive guilt illusion that such work is damaging to their families.

When queried about the future, these women say they want options. They want their choices validated—those that choose at some point to stay at home as well as those that aspire to reach the pinnacles of business careers and also have families.

These women told us they want time, help, compassion and appreciation for the unique value of their distinctly feminine contribution. They want a mature recognition of the variety of life available to both men and women, so that they are not forced to make decisions between career and family. Moreover, they want those decisions to be evolving and dynamic.

Women want corporations, organizations and families to support them. They want institutional and individual attitudes to be respectful of women's contributions and constraints.

They want recognition of the simple fact that women always have been and will continue to be the gender that bears children. It is not a question of fairness. It is simply a moot acknowledgement of the survival of the human species. They want sensitivity to childbearing and childcare issues. There are nearly thirty-three million women in the United States who have children under the age of eighteen. Sixty-five percent of these mothers are participants in the work force. Thirty-four million children have mothers who are working or seeking employment. For many women in our society to work or not to work is not the issue. It is the conditions of work and the right to succeed according to their abilities about which they speak.

Women have different needs from men—both biologically and psychologically. They need different kinds of flexibility, different environments in which to flourish, different supports, and different models. Successful, married, working women with children tell us that some of their problems are external, but much of the price they pay is internal struggle because of unmet needs. In spite of this, they have made major contributions to business life. They have redefined balance and attracted attention to needed restructuring of societal patterns, altering them for both women and men.

These women want their differences appreciated. According to the successful women with whom we talked, women work differently. Differences of nurturing, bonding, and cooperation could and should be instrumental—not incidental—in women's and institutions' successes. The women of the nineties want a new emphasis on a feminine success style embracing consensus and cooperation.

History parallels this theme.

We have moved from the aggressive, independent and paternalistic '40s and '50s in our nation's history to the '80s discussions of arms reduction, common markets, multinationals and, hopefully, an embracing of diversity in the '90s.

There is clarity and truth in the view suggesting that women and business will be better served by incorporating the same qualities which have made the women in this survey so successful: originality, emotion, cooperation, relationship-orientation, nurturing, empathy and female perspective. Certainly it illuminates a clearer path than in present policies of segregation.

Among discriminatory policies and ideas, such theories as the "Mommy Track" give signals that women who desire full family lives should not reach the top of business and organizations. Our best hope for the future is not in these negative theories and practices, but in the women who refuse to accept them and continue to optimistically reach for the highest ranks. The women who speak from the pages of this book have achieved success. Most are married, and all are mothers—as well as hardworking high achievers. There are important lessons to be learned from these women. They can provide models and inspirations to other women who aspire to career success and want a full, family life as well—the same life that men have aspired to throughout the ages without question of their rights to succeed and participate.

Women of the '90s do not expect pat answers, but they do want public discussion of what works and what doesn't work in addressing the enormously complicated and changing social dynamics of working, married women with children.

Today there is confusion over myths and realities. There are myths about women's aspirations and their ability to be mothers and career successes at the same time.

There are myths about who bears the costs and exactly what these costs are. There are individual costs to women struggling privately to define new roles. There are hidden costs to organizations in terms of retention, turnover and under-utilization. There are realistic fears of backlash and retreat. Many women and organizations accept self-imposed mythical limitations on the ability of women who are mothers to rise in entrepreneurial and organizational life and wield meaningful power.

The social realities of the '90s call for new career profiles to be created, so that married, working women with children can fully participate and aspire to wherever their talents, desires and commitments take them. Such women will need real *control* over their private and business lives in order to facilitate the delicate balance they must maintain. They will need real *power* from which to broker this control.

The pioneering spirit of the superachiever mommies whose stories—and successes—are presented in this book is a metaphor for the ability of the fabric of our whole system to succeed in offering meaningful options to all its members—women and men.

In looking to the future, we can not move backward. We should not sidetrack. Instead we need to move forward so that we can offer all our children—male and female— the care and the opportunities they deserve.

Bibliography

Adams, Jane, *Women on Top: Success Patterns and Personal Growth.* Hawthorne Books, New York, 1976.

Allman, S.L. and Grossman, F.K., Women's Career Plans and Maternal Employment. *Psychology of Women Quarterly,* Vol. 1, No. 4, Summer 1977.

Anderson, P.R. The Motive to Avoid Success and Instructional Set. 1974 ERIC p. 14 ED 098 470; MF.

Appleton, H.L., and Gurwitz, S.B., Willingness to Help as Determined by the Sex Role Appropriateness of the Help Seekers Career Goals. *Sex Roles,* Vol. 2, No. 4, 1977 pp. 321–330.

Bachtold, Louise, Personality Characteristics of Women of Distinction. *Psychology of Women Quarterly,* Fall 1976, Vol. 1, No. 1, pp. 70–78.

Bardwick, Judith, M. *Psychology of Women: A Study of Bio-Cultural Conflicts.* Harper & Row, Publishers, New York, 1971.

Barling, J., Fullagar, C. and March-Dingle, J., Employment commitment as a moderator of the maternal employment status/child behavior relationship. *Journal of Organization Behavior,* Apr. Vol. 9(2), pp. 113–122 (1988).

Barnett, R., Baruch, G., Women's involvement in multiple roles and psychological distress. *Journal of Personality and Social Psychology,* Jul. Vol. 49(1), pp. 135–145 (1985).

Baruch, G., Barnett, R., Role quality, multiple role involvement, and psychological well being in midlife women. *Journal of Personality and Social Psychology,* Sept. Vol. 51(3), 578–585. (1986).

Bem, Sandra. On the Utility of Alternative Procedures for Assessing Psychological Androgyny. *Journal of Consulting and Clinical Psychology,* 1977, Vol. 45, No. 2, pp. 196–105.

Bem, Sandra. Sex Role Adaptability: One Consequence of Psychological Androgyny. *Journal of Personality and Social Psychology,* 1975, Vol. 34, No. 5, pp. 1016–1023.

Bem, Sandra. Sex Typing and Androgyny; Further Explorations of the Expressive Domain. *Journal of Personality and Social Psychology.* 1976, Vol. 34, No. 5 pp. 1016–1023.

Bem, Sandra. Sex Typing and the Avoidance of Cross-Sex Behavior. *Journal of Personality and Social Psychology,* 1976, Vol. 33, No. 1, pp. 48–54.

Bem, Sandra. The Measurement of Psychological Androgyny. *Journal of Counselling and Clinical Psychology,* 1974, Vol. 42, No. 2, 155–162.

Bose, Utpala, Child Rearing attitudes of working and non-working mothers. *Psychological Research Journal,* Vol. 9(2), 54–61 (1985).

Broverman, I.K., Broverman, D.M., Clarkson, F.E., Rosenkrantz, P., and Vogel, S.R. Sex Role Stereotypes: A Current Appraisal. *Journal of Social Issues,* 28:2 (1972) pp. 59–78.

Bureau of Labor Statistics, *Occupational Outlook Handbook.* 1980–81 Edition, U.S. Department of Labor, March 1980, Bulletin 2075.

Chase-Lansdale, L. and Owen, M., Maternal employment in a family context: Effects on infant-mother and infant-father attachments. *Child Development,* Dec. Vol. 58(6), 1505–1512 (1987).

Cox, Linda Joyce, *Women; Work Role Conflict and Stress.* Ph.D Dissertation, U.C.L.A. 1985.

Cramer, S., Keitel, M. and Rossbery, R., The family and employed mothers. *International Journal of Family Psychiatry,* Vol. 7(1), 17–34 (1986).

Crockenberg, S., Stress and role satisfaction experienced by employed and non-employed mothers with young children. *Lifestyles* Summer Vol. 9(2), 97–110 (1988).

DeMeis, D., Hock, E. and McBride, S., The balance of employment and motherhood: Longitudinal study of mothers' feelings about separation from the first born infants.

Developmental Psychology, Sept. Vol. 22(5), 627–632 (1986).

Douban, Elizabeth. The Role of Models in Women's Professional Development. *Psychology of Women Quarterly.* Vol. 1, No. 1, Fall 1976 5–20.

Easterbrooks, M. and Goldberg, W., Effects of early maternal employment on toddlers, mothers and fathers. *Developmental Psychology*, Sept. Vol. 2(5), 774–783 (1985).

Employment and Training Report of the President. U.S. Government Printing Office. Washington, D.C., 1977.

Epstein, Cynthia, Fuchs, *Encountering the Male Establishment: Sex Status Limits* 9650982, 1970.

Epstein, Cynthia, Fuchs, *Woman's Place; Options and Limits in Professional Careers.* University of California Press, Berkeley, 1970.

Feather, N.T., Effects of Prior Success and Failure on Expectations of Success and Subsequent Performance. *Journal of Personality and Social Psychology.* 1966, 3, 287–298.

Feather, N.T., and Simon, J.G., Stereotypes of Male and Female Success and Failure at Sex Linked Occupations. *Journal of Personality*, March 1976, 44, 16–37.

Fraker, Susan, Why Women Aren't Getting to the Top. *Fortune* April 1984.

Gardner, K. and LaBrecque, S., Effects of maternal employment on sex role orientation of adolescents. *Adolescence*, Winter Vol. 21(84), 875–885 (1986).

Gilligan, Carol. *In a Different Voice.* Harvard University Press, Boston, 1982.

Goertzel, M.G., Goertzel, V., and Goertzel, T.G., *Three Hundred Eminent Personalities: A Psychosocial Analysis of the Famous.* Jossey-Bass 1982.

Helson, Ravenna, The Changing Image of the Career Woman. *Journal of Social Issues*, 28:2 (1972) pp. 33–46.

Hennig, Margaret, and Jardim, Anne. *The Managerial Woman.* Simon and Schuster, New York, 1976.

Herman, J.B., and Kuczynski, K.A., *The Professional Women; Inter and Intra Role Conflict.* 1973 ERIC, 22p CED (718 MF).

Hoffman, L., Effects of maternal employment in the two-parent family. *American Psychologist,* Feb. Vol. 44(2), 283–292 (1989).

Hoffman, L.W. Fear of Success in Males and Females 1965 and 1971. *Journal of Consulting and Clinical Psychology,* 42:3 (1974), pp. 353–358.

Hoffman, L.W. Early Childhood Experiences and Women's Achievement Motives. *Journal of Social Issues,* 28:2 1972 pp. 129–155.

Holter, H. *Sex Roles and Social Structure.* Oslo: Universite-forlaget. 1970.

Horner, M.S. Toward an Understanding of Achievement-Related Conflicts in Women. *Journal of Social Issues.* 1972, 28, 157–175.

Kanter, Rosabeth Moss *Men and Women of the Corporation.* Basic Books Inc., New York. 1977.

Karen, Robert, Becoming Attached. *The Atlantic,* February 1990.

Kaufman: Debra & Barbara Richardson. *Achievement and Women: Challenging the Assumptions.* The Free Press, New York, 1982.

Kiger, G., Working women and their children. *Social Science Journal,* Oct Vol. 21(4), 49–57 (1984).

Korn/Ferry. International Graduate School of Management, UCLA. 1982.

Krause, N., Employment outside the home and women's psychological well-being. *Social Psychiatry,* Vol. 19(1), 41–48 (1984).

Lockheed, Marlaine E., Female Motive to Avoid Success. A Psychological Barrier or a Response to Deviancy. *Sex Roles,* Vol. 1, No. 1, 1975.

McLaughlin, M., Cormier, S. and Cormier, W., Relation between coping strategies and distress, stress and marital adjustment of multiple-role women. *Journal of Counseling Psychology*, Apr. Vol. 35(2), 187–193 (1988).

Mednick, Martha Tamara, et al., (Ed.) *Women and Achievement: Social and Motivational Analysis.* Hemisphere Publishing Corporation, Washington, 1975.

Oppenheimer, Valerie K. The Sex-Labeling of Jobs. *Industrial Relations,* 7 (3) 219–234, 1968.

Pietromonaco, P., Manis, J. and Frohardt, K., Psychological consequences of multiple social roles. *Psychology of Women Quarterly,* Dec. Vol. 10(4), 373–381 (1986).

Ritchie, J., Child rearing practices and attitudes of working and full-time mothers. *Women's Studies-International Forum,* Vol. 5(5), 419–425 (1982).

Schmidt, Warren H., Barry Posner. Managerial Values in Perspective An AMA Survey Report. AMA Membership Publications Division, New York, 1983.

Schwartz, F., Management women and the new facts of life. *Harvard Business Review,* Jan–Feb 1989 Num 1.

Stein, A.H. and Bailey, M.M. The Socialization of Achievement Orientation in Females. *Psychological Bulletin,* 973, 80, 345–366.

Suchet, M. and Barling, J., Employed mothers: Interrole conflict, spouse support and marital functioning. *Journal of Occupational Behavior,* Jul. Vol. 7(3), 167–178 (1986).

Tangri, S.S. Determinants of Occupational Role Innovation Among College Women. *Journal of Social Issues,* 28:2 (1972) pp. 177–199.

Vaillant, George E. *Adaptation to Life.* Little, Brown, Boston, 1977.

Venkatarama, H., Professional employment of mothers: Impact on personality and parent-child interaction. *Journal of Indian Psychology,* Jan–Jul Vol. 6, 13–23 (1987).

Wall Street Journal/Gallup Survey. Wall Street Journal, 1984. Dow Jones & Company.

"Recommended Corporate Policies for Working Mothers," *Parents*, Women Employed Institute, Chicago, Illinois.

"Report of the Dual Career Project," Resource: Careers.

"Facts on Working Women-Current Population Survey," U.S. Dept. of Labor Women's Bureau, March 1988.